The Charlton
Standard Catalogue of

Canadian
Country Store
Collectables

Second Edition

By
**Bill and Pauline Hogan
and Ed Locke**

W.K. Cross
Publisher

The Charlton Press

Birmingham, Michigan ● Toronto, Ontario

Canadian Cataloguing in Publication Data

The Charlton standard catalogue of country store collectables

Biennial.
2nd ed. -
Continues a publication issued under title: Canadian
country store collectalbes, published in 1979
ISSN 1208-9230
ISBN 0-88968-184-8 (1997 ed.)

1. Antiques- -Canada- -Catalogs. 2. Collectibles- -
Canada- -Catalogs. 3. Commercial art- - Canada- -
Catalogs. 4. General stores- -Collectibles- -Canada
Catalogs.

NK1133.C45   745.1'029'471   C97-900094-7

Printed in Canada
in the Province of Quebec

The Charlton Press

Editorial Office
2040 Yonge Street, Suite 208
Toronto, Ontario M4S 1Z9

EDITORIAL

Editor   Nicola Leedham

Graphic Technician   Davina Rowan

ACKNOWLEDGEMENTS

The Charlton Press wishes to thank those who have helped and assisted with this revised and expanded edition of *The Charlton Standard Catalogue of Canadian Country Store Collectables*.

CONTRIBUTORS

Our thanks to those who assisted in the research for the Macdonald and Davidson article: Jonathan Pottel, Montreal; Doug Wood, Toronto: Metro Toronto Public Library reference department; St. Catharines Public Library reference department; GSW Limited. Our thanks also to the photographers: Frank Torelli, Bill Borgwardt and Rob Gordon. With thanks to the collectors who shared their treasures: Bill Borgwardt; Jim Close; Jowe and Pauline Creighton; Barbara and Rollo McDonald; Mike and Shirley Roberts; John Sebert; Mary Elizabeth and Stroman Watford; Greg Williams; and Frank Williams. Thanks also to *Tin Type* magazine for the Master Mason photograph.

A SPECIAL NOTE TO COLLECTORS

The Charlton Press has an ongoing commitment to excellence and completeness in the production of all its reference works. Your help in providing new or previously unobtainable data on any aspect of Country Store collecting will be considered for inclusion in subsequent editions. Those providing information will be acknowledged in the contributor's section of this catalogue.

Please send your contributions together with your name, address and phone number to our editorial offices in Toronto:

Editorial Office:
2040 Yonge Street, Suite 208
Toronto, Ontario M4S 1Z9
Telephone: (416) 488-1418 Fax: (416) 488-4653
Telephone: (800) 442-6042 Fax: (800) 442-1542

CONTENTS

ABOUT THE AUTHORS

Pauline and Bill Hogan bring a wealth of personal knowledge to the subject of Canadian country store collecting. They have travelled extensively in Canada and the United States searching for artifacts and for information about them. They possess some of the finest of Canadian country store memorabilia. Bill has presented lectures to historical societies and antique classes, appeared on television to discuss Canadian collectables and he and Pauline have prepared articles for Canadian and American collectors' journals. In real life Bill is a full-time antique dealer and show promoter. After a career in teaching, Pauline is working on a master's degree in Religious Studies at McMaster University.

Ed Locke has been a full-time nostalgia, advertising and toy dealer for twenty-five years. The partnership of Ed and his wife, Sheryl, Locke and MacKenzie, does up to 36 shows a year across Canada and the United States. Ed and Sheryl also own some of the finest Canadian artifacts, especially in advertising. In recent years Ed has started a successful auction house, immediately attracting top country store merchandise and setting record prices. He has been involved in show promotion right from the beginning of his antique career, and is currently a partner in the Toronto Collectibles Extravaganza Show.

PREFACE TO THE 1979 EDITION

About three or four years ago, tins, signs, and other advertising items started appearing at the specialty "bottle shows" in Ontario, British Columbia and Alberta, and a boom in "country store" collectables started. We became intrigued with the items, first for their value as decor, and then for their own sake. Thus began an engrossing spare time and weekend hobby, which has taken us all over Ontario, into Quebec and the United States, and into the homes of many other collectors. Some people, like ourselves, began collecting the whole range of artifacts from the smallest advertising buttons to the largest coffee mill. Others made a specialty out of just one area of interest, tobacco tins, for example, or thermometers or sewing stuff. Today, collectors from across the country, from advertising directors to ten-year-old students, collect these country store artifacts. As well, "theme" restaurants like Mother's Pizza parlours and Crock and Block, (and I hear, McDonald's in the near future) have introduced country store collectables to the public at large and have created a brand new interest.

The term "country store collectable" is not terribly accurate. Actually we mean "general store" because, of course, the old city stores had the same attractive stuff. The connotation of a country store, however, with its hint of nostalgia, variety, and warmth, conveys the attraction of this kind of collecting. It includes advertising — posters, trade cards, and all sorts of give-away items which range from stuffed dolls to small furniture, all imprinted with a commercial message. It also includes store fixtures like coffee mills, dispensers, large bins, mirrors, and so on, and the ones with a commercial message are preferable. It also includes the containers and sometimes the contents that were sold in an old general store. Anything, in fact that is pleasant to look at, to display, or to wonder about, and that recalls an older, less sophisticated time is a collectable. In general, the better the graphics of the design of the piece, the more beautiful it is, and therefore, the more valuable.

The era of the country store collectable is fairly recent. Up until the 19th century, the needs of rural dwellers were met by peddlers. Eventually, as roads were improved and the population thickened, small crossroads communities with, characteristically, a store, a post office, and perhaps a blacksmith, would serve these needs instead.

The 19th century also saw the development of canning techniques and techniques for lithographing on tin-plated steel. Thus, producers could package their goods in pleasing containers designed to attract the eye in the crowded store and also suitable for long term storage, transportation, and home use.

All these developments produced the highly attractive containers and advertising pieces we treasure today. These collectables date, therefore, from about the mid-19th century to about the 20th. The cut-off date at this end can be quite a personal thing: whenever you feel "old" ends and "contemporary" begins. Generally, if your grandparents might have used it, it's charmingly collectable, but if you can remember it, you're not so charmed.

Canadian collectors have been working in a vacuum. Very few correspond, largely because they don't know each other and because Canadians don't have the advantage of large advertising shows, like the American ones in Gaithersburg or Indianapolis, that let you know if you have significant pieces in your collection or ones that are quite common (but personally pleasing). We hope this book changes some of that. There are enough really good items illustrated and described in the book to spur on the serious collector. The larger selection of the more common artifacts will help the beginning collector (or antique dealer) buy with a greater measure of security in a sometimes bewildering market place. All the items are Canadian, or, as in the case of the coffee mills and Diamond Dye cabinets, used in Canadian stores as well as American ones.

This book is not meant to be an encyclopedia of Canadian country store collectables. Many items can be found which are not illustrated. However, with careful study, the book can serve as an excellent guide to the value of un-catalogued pieces.

We hope this book will serve as a spur to new collectors to seek out and rescue many of these artifacts from the basements and attics of old country stores in their areas. The hobby is young enough that undoubtedly the best pieces are still to come.

PREFACE TO THE SECOND EDITION

Canadian Country Store Collectables was originally written in 1979 in response to a growing need for information, any information, on a new collectable category of antiques. It was never intended to be an encyclopedia of country store items nor was it to be the last word on the subject. However, seventeen years later it is still the Bible of this collecting category and the authors regularly receive requests for copies. In response to this, Charlton Press decided to publish a second edition of the book, with an eye to further books on the subject to form a comprehensive library of Canadian Country Store Collectables. This revised edition contains about 50 additions not included in the original book. The chapter on decorating has been deleted. To bring the price guide up to date, Ed Locke, a leading Canadian country store dealer and collector has received advice from other dealers and collectors across Canada.

Country store collecting has really come of age since 1979. The "Starting a Collection" chapter to the 1979 edition (reprinted here) seems so naive. Yes, at that time, there were old stores with attics undisturbed for fifty years. But today at least if you want to collect tins or signs you can find dealers handling them. All major antique shows have a "nostalgia" dealer or two in their line-up, and the big outdoor shows have many.

Prices have come a very long way too, since 1979. The publishing of the 1979 book set off a huge demand for porcelain signs, especially "kitchen" ones, and the 1996 prices reflect this. The 1982 auction of the Black Cat clock for $7,500 legitimized country store collecting for many in Canada and one of those clocks recently changed hands in Canada for over $20,000.

Perhaps the most shocking thing resulting from the original publication of the book is the realization that some of these artifacts are extremely rare. It was presumed that the book would bring onto the market a lot of items, perhaps even drive prices down. No way! Only a couple of the 3 Strikes tins have been found, only a few Black Cat clocks, and there is still only one "Before and After" Tucketts paper-under-glass. In 1979, the introduction expressed a hope that the hobby was young enough that "the best pieces are still to come." From a 1996 vantage point, this isn't quite as assured as it was then.

One final note. This revised edition has changed the catalogue numbers into an alphabetical listing for ease of research. The original numbers reflected the quality of an item. The best tobacco tins were listed first, the best sign first in the sign category. We hope this change to alphabetical order assists the reader.

Oh, one more thing. Just as we said in 1979 — leave us just a few more things.

Bill and Pauline Hogan and Ed Locke
September, 1996

INTRODUCTION

Starting A Collection (1979)

The essence of collecting anything, it seems, is to search for and then own objects that give you pleasure. The next step, though, seems to be owning objects that not only give pleasure but are also valuable. Why worth has to play any part in the game of collecting is something we don't know, but we do know it does play a part for us, for friends in collecting and for thousands of people who will buy a book with a price guide but wouldn't buy a copy of the same collecting book if the price guide weren't included. The great dream of stamp collectors (and art collectors?) is to find that great piece, that super rarity, in someone's basement, or in grandma's attic or in the ignored collection of a friend. It never happens in stamps. At least we know it has never happened to us or anyone we know, but it happens all the time to people who collect country store items. What follows is a guide on how to put together a worthwhile collection of country store items without a lot of money

To start with, collecting country store items is such a new field that there *are* still treasures to be found in attics and basements. While people have been looking for Kreighoff paintings or the British Guiana penny stamp for a hundred years, the hunt for country store collectables has just started.

Go to local stores that look old and tell the owner what you're after and ask if he or she will look for some old artifacts for you. It doesn't matter if you're in the city or the country. Every area has old stores with attics undisturbed for fifty years. The promise of money for useless junk opens many a closed door. One hint — buy the first item offered even if it is useless to you. This sets up a better rapport, gets the adrenaline going, and makes the owner want to continue looking.

If you can't find things at the source, the old stores, then get them from the next best place — the flea market dealer. Most of Canada now has a flea market somewhere nearby. Visit it regularly. Let every dealer know what you're looking for — tins, signs or whatever — leave your phone number or else promise to return every week or every two weeks to see if something has come up. Follow up. Sometimes dealers will pass up good items in basements just because they seem too expensive but will go back and buy when you say *any* porcelain door push is worth ten dollars to you and you'll pay more if you like it.

Another way to get a good collection is to tell everybody you know that you collect this old junk. Sooner or later someone will have a grandfather who had a store or someone will know that the contents of a store you didn't know about are going to be auctioned off next Tuesday evening.

So much for getting a good collection cheaply. Now, if you're really serious and don't mind paying somewhere near what things are worth, you can visit shows. Most antique shows have a dealer or two who brings in some nostalgia or country store things. Again, tell the dealers what your are looking for so they will buy these things when they see them. Most parts of Canada also have specialty nostalgia shows. They seem to have grown out of bottle shows and so

may still be advertised as such but there are usually some tins or advertising pieces among the articles for sale.

A few hints for buying at shows. Most dealers expect you to bargain and so price things accordingly. Roughly, there's always 10% off. Occasionally you can get more off. Sometimes even a firm price becomes a bit cheaper by the end of a show.

A note of warning though: never bargain a bargain. If a dealer brings in a very good tin that should be worth $20 and you bargain him from eight dollars to five, you're looking for trouble. When he finds out the value, and he will, he'll be especially irritated at the extra loss he took and will always feel enmity towards you. Not only will you never get a discount from him again, but he'll speak about you for years to other dealers just because of the one incident. It would have been much better to pleasantly say that you liked the tin and then buy it. You have no obligation of offer more — even if the item is worth much more than you paid for it. Any person claiming to be a dealer by setting up articles with prices on them should do the proper research before putting something out for sale. When that dealer finds out he has sold you a twenty dollar tin for eight dollars, he should only rue the fact that he didn't get as much money as he should have, he shouldn't bear the buyer any malice.

A few other hints for collecting. Always buy the best. Don't buy four junky things instead of one good one. Don't buy damaged items when mint ones are available, despite the huge price difference. A scratched and rusty five dollar tin will be worth five dollars in three years. A mint fifteen dollar tin will be worth twenty-five dollars. Mint things are always easier to sell later on as well.

So, you now know where to get the country store items and you know you're only supposed to collect things in good condition but you like everything in this book and you don't know what to collect first? Start with things that are functional. We use the Lyman's box on page 67 as a coffee table and the Corticelli cabinet on page 13 as an end table. They mean a lot more to us than many of the more valuable items we have in the collection room downstairs. The tins, the miller sign and the framed labels we keep in the kitchen are "special" to us and we enjoy looking at them. Decorative functional items abound in the country store field and are both cheap and easy to come by.

After buying something functional, it is probably a good idea to buy anything that you like the looks of. Sooner or later, when you are sure of what you really like, you can set about gathering in earnest. If you specialize too early — such as collecting only one pound coffee canisters — you will lose interest as soon as it gets tough to find anymore, and that will be soon. After all, the main aim is to build a collection, not just sit with four items. At last count our collection had about fifteen categories. We never go to a show without finding something, even it it's only a pin-back button, and usually we add a half a dozen new items. That makes it all fun, and that's the essence of collecting, isn't it?

So, have fun, but leave us just a few more things.

How To Use This Price Guide

This price guide is just that — a guide only. It is not meant to be a guarantee or a promise or anything more than a helpful aid to buying and selling country store items in Canada. Many of the items are too rare for a perfectly accurate appraisal of their worth. You may know that at a farm auction a certain item sold for twice the amount listed. Or, you may write us and claim that you've had a tin in your antique store for three months at half the listed price and it hasn't sold. Both of these extremes are commonplace and can't be helped.

The premise for this guide is that all articles are in good condition and are offered for sale at an antique or nostalgia show by someone who wants to sell. The prices listed are what the dealer should expect to get. A collector paying these prices is getting fair value. A person selling items to a dealer should reasonably expect to get about half value for the lower priced ones and somewhat more than half for items valued over $100. It is possible that a collector would pay much more than these prices.

A few more guiding words. We are using only three descriptive terms for condition:

Excellent refers to a piece that is in near-mint condition with very few signs of minor wear.

Good refers to a piece that displays well but does show signs of wear.

Fair refers to a piece that is worn enough to be just OK for a collection.

On a scale of 10 (with 10 being mint), these terms would equal 9, 7, and 5 respectively.

It should also be noted that prices can vary from one region of Canada to another. A tin that is common in B.C. might be uncommon in Ontario. Hudson Bay Company items, for example, are more highly valued in the west than in the Maritimes.

Items must look good to have value. Rust on the face of a tin makes it unacceptable. Spool cabinets with drawers missing are unacceptable; porcelain signs with big chips are unacceptable. All prices quoted are the opinions of the authors only, although advice has been considered from colleagues across Canada. We cannot be held responsible for any loss, real or imagined, that occurs from using this price guide, nor do we expect to share any unexpected profits.

All items are measured in centimetres, width by height by depth.

Catalogue Numbers

In this revised edition of *Canadian Country Store Collectables* we have changed the catalogue numbering system of the first book. The categories have been re-organized alphabetically with a "Miscellaneous" section at the end. The items in each category are similarly arranged alphabetically by brand name. The name of the manufacturer, where known, appears underneath the brand name. The exception to this is the tobacco tin section where the manufacturer's name precedes the brand name. The tobacco manufacturers are listed in alphabetical order, for example The Imperial Tobacco Company follows B. Houde and Company, and the brands produced by each manufacturer are listed together. At the end of the major tobacco manufacturers there is a section of private labels which are listed alphabetically by brand name.

Each category has its own abbreviation. For example, coffee tins are "CT," dispensers and displays are "D," mirrors are "MIR," and tobacco tins are "TT."

CT-3, therefore, would refer to the third one in an alphabetical arrangement of all the coffee tins in this edition.

Don't worry, you will grasp this easily once you use the book.

Shows

The following is a list of shows which have the greatest number of dealers selling country store collectables. If you know of any other shows which are not included here, please let us know and we will be sure to include them in our next edition.

Alberta
Calgary Summer Antiques Show, Canada Olympic Park, Calgary, AB. Contact Jeff Gadsden (519) 925-6606
The Wild Rose Antique Show Edmonton

Ontario
Christie Antique Show, Christie Conservation Area, Dundas, ON. Contact Jeff Gadsden (519) 925-6606
Flamboro, May through October at Aberfoyle, Barrie or Milton. Contact (905) 685-1225
Nostalgia-Rama Show, Fairgrounds Auditorium, Woodstock. Contact Bill Lavell (905) 278-7363 Fax (905) 278-4971
Odessa Antique Show and Sale. Contact Bill Dobson (613) 283-5270
Ottawa Nostalgia Show, Nepean Sportsplex, 1701 Woodruffe Ave. Contact Ken Aubrey (613) 738-1942
The Toronto Collectibles Extravaganza Show. Contact Ed Locke (613) 738-1942

Where to find Show Dates

There are more magazines than ever to tell you the dates of each show.

Antiques! Box 1860, Suite 702, 27 Queen Street East, Toronto, ON, M5C 2M6

Antiques and Collectables Trader P.O. Box 38095, 550 Eglinton Ave. W., Toronto, ON M5N 3A8

Antique Showcase 103 Lakeshore Rd. Suite 202, St. Catharines, ON L2N 2T6

The Charlton Collector's Guide to Ontario 2040 Yonge Street, Suite 204, Toronto, ON M4S 1Z9 provides a year-round source for shows throughout the province

The Upper Canadian Box 653, Smiths Falls, ON K7A 4T6

TWO TIN GODS: DAVIDSON AND MACDONALD

One of the things you notice when collecting Canadian tins is that one of two names, Thos. Davidson Mfg. Co., or the Macdonald Mfg. Co., usually appears in small type in the corners near the bottom of the container. These two companies, between them, dominated tin box manufacturing in Canada from the late 1800s until 1927.

The Thos. Davidson Manufacturing Company of Montreal, and the the Macdonald Manufacturing Company of Toronto, both grew from the creative spirit of immigrant Scots. Thomas Davidson and David Macdonald were both innovators, Macdonald in lithography and Davidson in enamelling. Each transformed his particular genius into commercial success, and they shared between them the growing market for tins in the rapidly expanding Canada of the turn of the century.

Thomas Davidson

Thomas Davidson arrived in Canada from Edinburgh in 1842, an 18 year old adventurer. We're not sure what he did for the next 10 years, but in 1852 he is listed as a clerk in the Montreal directory. His career really begins in 1858. It was then that he began working with William Darling, an iron and hardware merchant. Darling was married to a Miss Davidson from Edinburgh, so he may have been a relative. It was evidently while working for Darling that Davidson began learning about a new German process for bonding glass to metal, and started the first enamelling process to be done in Canada.

Davidson went into business for himself in 1860 as a hardware merchant. By 1865 he was advertising "Japanned and planished (flattened) and stamped tin goods," so he was obviously expanding the tinware part of his business. Japanning is the glossy black lacquering meant to resemble the imported Oriental painted chests so admired at the time.

For the next few years Davidson worked with partners. Robert Kerr joined him in 1866; Kerr's area of interest was household tools and stoves. The partners were now at 22 and 30 Hospital Street in Montreal. In 1869 a neighbour, Charles Storer, joined the firm, which became Dominion Stamping Works. Storer was the artist of the group; he specialized in fancy decoration and gilt lettering signs. The Dominion Stamping Works factory was in the the Albert, Delisle and Dominion Street district of Montreal. The Davidson business remained at this location.

The partnership broke up in 1871, and Thomas Davidson and Company was born. Davidson retained the name Dominion Stamping Works as well for his business, which reverted to stamping tin, iron and Britannia metal for a while, but by 1875 he was again advertising Japanning and hardware manufacturing.

Slowly the business expanded, and from 1875 on Davidson used a variety of different offices and showrooms, always keeping the factory at 187 Delisle. This was the era of stencilled tins, which do not bear a manufacturer's name. They are, therefore, difficult to assign to a particular company. Stencilling involved laying on a base colour,

usually red, green or black, and then using a contrasting colour, commonly gold, to simply paint on a label, using a stencil. By the 1890s lithography was being perfected, indeed the tin manufacturers were apparently the first to prove the effectiveness of the new technique. An early example of a Davidson lithographed tin is the Maharajah on page 134, which uses an interesting combination of the older stencilling technique and the newer lithography. The range of colours available through lithography must have seemed miraculous. Canadian tin manufacturers didn't adopt this new technique as quickly as the Americans and as a result there are tins lithographed for Canadian companies by American firms dating from the 1870s. The Davidson. Ritchie Co. St. Leger tin on page 180 is an example. It was lithographed by the Somers Bros. firm of Brooklyn, New York, in 1879.

In 1880 Davidson began taking his sons (Thomas, T. Charles and James) into partnership. In 1891 they had an office in Toronto, which explains why some Toronto companies used Davidson tins, the Todhunter on page 36 is an example. In 1894, Thomas Davidson died leaving behind him a thriving business that would go on to produce some of the most stunning tins ever seen in North America.

James, who had been forced to work his way up through the ranks of the company, took over as president and renamed it The Thomas Davidson Manufacturing Company Ltd. When trying to date a tin it is helpful to remember that Mfg and Ltd. appear with the Davidson name only after 1894. A lithographed tin bearing the name Thomas Davidson & Co. is an early one and was manufactured before 1894. Actually, most of the Davidson tins collected are Thos. Davidson Mfg. Co. Ltd. because manufacturer's names are not found on tins before the advent of lithography in the 1890s.

Under James Davidson, the company became one of the largest enamelling and stamping works in the country. By 1900 it had over 600 employees. They expanded their business and increased production of enamelled ware (granite ware) and other housewares. In 1910 the company received a gold medal at the Paris Exposition for some of the work it had manufactured. By 1906 Davidson had offices in Australia, New Zealand and South Africa as well as Winnipeg and Toronto. The opening up of Canada's west was a boon to the company and by 1927 it had branches in Saskatoon, Calgary and Vancouver.

In 1927 the Thomas Davidson Manufacturing Company merged with three other firms: The McClary Manufacturing Company, London, The Sheet Metal Products Company, and the Happy Thought Foundry Company of Brantford. The Sheet Metal Products Company had acquired the Macdonald Manufacturing Company several years earlier so the two big tin manufacturing companies were now part of a merged operation that was called General Steel Wares. The Davidson plant at 187 Delisle became the centre of the General Steel Wares housewares manufacturing complex. General Steel Wares' is now known as GSW.

David Macdonald

The other giant of tin manufacturing was the Macdonald Manufacturing Company of Toronto.

David Macdonald was born in 1837 in Arbroath, Scotland. He was a surgical artist for the Aberdeen Medical Academy before coming to Canada in 1870. He spent some time travelling through the United States— painting in California, and losing a trunk in New York which contained, among other things, letters from Queen Victoria. Macdonald married in Buffalo, and then came to Toronto in 1874. He is first mentioned in 1879 as a "plater," and then the next year, he entered into partnership with James Davies. Their plant at 231 King Street East manufactured "grocers" cannisters [sic], spice tins, biscuit boxes, etc." By 1882 Macdonald was alone in the business, which he renamed Victoria Tin Works.

In 1883 he moved his plant to Sherbourne Street and then in 1884 moved back to 231 King Street East. It is interesting to note that, from the beginning of his career, Macdonald preferred to have someone else handle the business side of the company's affairs while he attended to the actual manufacturing process. When the company was first formed, William Hughes was president and treasurer and Macdonald was manager.

Macdonald was an artist and designer. His obituary describes him as an expert in the process of lithography on tin plate. He was so involved in the factory that for several years he made his home above the plant. His household included two children and his father David Senior, who also worked at the plant, describing himself as a "tinsmith" one year, and an "engineer" the next.

The pre-1890 Macdonald tins are almost impossible to identify. The real interest lies in the way he used lithography. Some Macdonald tins use a combination of embossing and lithography. The 1899 Kodak on page 167 and the 1898 B. Houde Golden Leaf on page 150 are examples. Some tins use a combination of lithographed paper and lithography on tin, as in the Belfast Blend tea bin on page 128. This tin has an exceptionally fine decorative border detail. Other tins, using lithography on tin only, show equally fine detail and balance.

While Macdonald produced some of the finest advertising pieces known for other people, he did very little advertising himself. He took no ads in the city directory, and not until 1910 did he place an ad in the Canadian Trade Index. By then the company had offices in Toronto, Montreal and Winnipeg. They were making: "tins for biscuits, coffee, tea, blacking lye, syrup, starch, butter, oil, candy, tobacco, mustard, druggists' supplies, cough drops, ointment, dyes, uniform cases, baking powder, lard pails, dredge tins, tin signs for advertising lithographed of plain." Unlike Davidson, Macdonald never diversified beyond tin wares, and in fact, seemed to be proud of that. A 1910 advertisement promised "undivided attention" to the customer's special needs.

Macdonald had many friends among the inventors of his day. He received one of the first gramophones from Thomas Edison. His daughter, Marie Christine Shaw, recalls summers at their cottage on Trout Lake, when they would take their gramophone out to the shore of the lake and play music for all their neighbours. Macdonald was also a friend of Thomas, of the Thomas Flyer — an early automobile — and he bought the first model. He was so fond of the car that he took it with him on many of his frequent trips to Scotland.

Macdonald remained involved with his company until about 1910, although in 1896 William Tassie took over as manager. He devoted more time to painting in his later years, and was friends with the Group of Seven. A Continental Can employee maintains that some members of the Group of Seven designed tins as part of the commercial work they did. Canadian humourist Greg Clark was another of David Macdonald's famous friends. David Macdonald died on April 3, 1921.

The Macdonald plant was situated at 231 King Street East until 1896 when it moved to King and Simcoe. It became Macdonald Mfg. Co. Ltd. in 1901 and in 1905 moved to 143-145 Spadina. In 1911 the Kemp Manufacturing Co. of Toronto acquired the Macdonald Manufacturing Company. The Kemp company then changed its name to Sheet Metal Products, but continued to operate the Macdonald company under its own name. In 1927, Sheet Metal Products was one the companies which merged to form General Steel Wares, which also continued to operate Macdonald as a wholly-owned subsidiary. Macdonald now had a factory in Winnipeg as well as Toronto. In 1944 the Macdonald company was sold to Continental Can Company of Canada and the Macdonald Manufacturing Company finally disappeared.

Dating Tins

Dating the tins which were produced at the Davidson plant is sometimes easy, sometimes impossible. It's easy when the manufacturer indicates on the tin the date the design was registered. Sometimes this date is found beside the manufacturer's name; other times it may be cleverly set into the design. If the date is not given, you must look for other clues and here a history of the manufacturer is important. Stencilled tins which have no manufacturer's name are generally pre-1890. Lithographed tins with Thos. Davidson and Co. are 1890-1894.

Davidson tins manufactured after the death of Thomas Davidson in 1894 are labelled "The Thomas Davidson Manufacturing Company Ltd." or "Limited."

Dating Macdonald tins follows many of the same rules used in dating Davidson tins. Stencilled tins are the earliest, but impossible to identify for sure as Macdonald. The very earliest lithographed tins carry a large and prominent address: 231 King Street East. The Choice Family Tea tin on page 129 is an example. These tins had to be no later than 1896. Between that year and 1901, tins were labelled "Macdonald M''f'g. Co.," after 1901 you find "Macdonald Mfg. Co. Limited."

As a general rule the appearance of the tin gives you some clues as to its age. Embossing is generally limited to the 1895-1900 period. The older tins have more detailed designs and engravings. Compare the Red Rose Tea on page 136 with the Heavy Draught on page 130, a much earlier tin. Sometimes you may be lucky and find a date on the tin, and that's the best way to pinpoint its age.

There are surprises in the histories of the Macdonald Manufacturing Company and the Davidson Manufacturing Company. David Macdonald did not run his own company during the years when the most collectable tins were being manufactured — 1895 to 1920. Thomas Davidson was not involved at all in the heyday of tins. His son James was guiding the company by then. And, although we've concentrated on their tin production, the Thomas Davidson Company actually put more emphasis on its enamelled wares — granite ware and household appliances — than it did on the manufacture of tins. Despite this, these two companies were the giants of the tin box industry at the turn of the century.

The tins produced by Davidson and Macdonald are superb and may be the best in the world. *Tin Type,* the magazine for tin collectors, stated: "Canadian tins are available which seriously challenge and often surpass even the very best, and very rarest, American-made tins." Words

like "spectacular" are used to describe the Gold Dust on page 157, the Taxi on page 160, the Master Mason on page 168 and the Poker on page 169. The Gold Dust is a Davidson tin, and while the other three are unmarked, they were probably produced by either Davidson or Macdonald.

The two companies often seemed to be trying to outdo one another. If Davidson put out an unusually attractive tin, Macdonald often followed with something as nice. The McLaren's coffee bin by Macdonald on page 34 and the Todhunter bin on page 36 by Davidson are one example of this apparent competitiveness. Look too at the two starch tins, Lily White on page 47 by Macdonald and Crystal Gloss on page 45 by Davidson.

Canadian tin collectors owe a great deal to the Macdonald Manufacturing Company and the Thomas Davidson Manufacturing Company. The quantity of tins they produced provides a ready supply, and the excellence of design and workmanship make collecting these tins a rewarding pastime. If you have one of the better tins manufactured by either company, you know you have one of the finest tins ever made.

Agricultural

BEST HOOF
Domestic Speciality Co. Limited

NONSUCH
Nonsuch Mfg. Co. Limited

Nonsuch was a manufacturer of leather polishes and dressings. This is a Macdonald tin.

Cat. No.	Description	Dimensions	F	G	Ex
AGR-1	Best Hoof Ointment	9 x 9	25.00	40.00	75.00
AGR-2	Nonsuch Harness Oil	12.5 diameter	20.00	40.00	75.00

SUCCESS MANURE SPREADER
Paris Plough Company

The Paris Plough Company of Paris, Ontario issued this tiny tray. It is said that Mackenzie King once spoke from the back of a manure spreader while campaigning in rural Canada. He declared, "I never thought I'd speak from a Tory platform."

Cat. No.	Description	Dimensions	F	G	Ex
AGR-3	Tip Tray		60.00	150.00	300.00

Apothecary

ALLEN'S LUNG BALSAM
Allen's

DEGUIRE COUGH DROPS
T. Deguire

The frame to the Allen's window has hinge marks, so the piece was probably the front of a cabinet in a drugstore. Allen's Lung Balsam came from Montreal and was a very popular remedy in Canada for "consumption," a catch-all name for half a dozen maladies.

The Thos. Davidson Co. of Montreal produced this cough drop tin. The odd shape and the lithographed picture of the factory mark this tin as exceptional. Tins with factory scenes are popular with collectors. Many companies proudly pictured their factory on the front of the tin as if to display their prosperity and thus instill confidence in the product.

Cat. No.	Description	Dimensions	F	G	Ex
AP-1	Allen's Lung Balsam Window	35 x 75	400.00	1000.00	1500.00
AP-2	Deguire Cough Drops	20 X 11	25.00	60.00	100.00

EGYPTIAN BOUQUET
Watkins

DR. KELLOG'S
Northrop & Lyman Co.

Talc tins are extremely collectable.

Dr. J. D. Kellog's Asthma Remedy was a popular product, even at the 1900 price of $1 for a small tin. The powder was burned — often on the lift-off lid of the can — and inhaled through a "chimney."

Cat. No.	Description	Dimensions	F	G	Ex
AP-3	Egyptian Bouquet	7 x 13.5	10.00	30.00	45.00
AP-4	Dr. Kellog's Asthma Remedy	6.5 x 12.5	10.00	20.00	30.00

IMPERIAL COUGH DROPS
R & T Watson

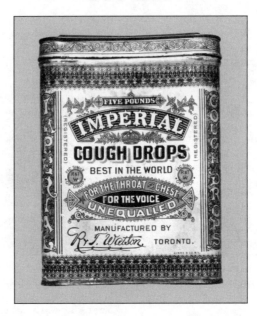

The tin containing Watson's Imperial Cough Drops is a rarity because it was made for a Canadian company by the American firm Ginna and Co. of New York. It therefore predates 1901, when Ginna was bought out by American Can Company. Watson promises that their cough drops are "invaluable to orators and vocalists."

Cat. No.	Description	Dimensions	F	G	Ex
AP-5	Imperial Cough Drops	15.5 x 20	20.00	40.00	60.00

LYMAN'S
The Lyman Bros.& Co. Limited

MENNEN'S
Gerhard Mennen Chemical Co.

Undoubtedly the most colourful tin ever made in Canada! The front, sides, slope-front and even the back are lithographed in brilliant reds, golds, and blues. The tin is quite large and evidently a whole bank of them would face a potential customer. This one held "dark" cough drops. As scarce as the tin is, the Niagara-on-the-Lake Apothecary Shop proudly displays four of them.

Talcum powder tins have become highly collectable, due mainly to the smiling babies featured. The child on the Mennen tin was the son of one of the company's employees. Mr. Mennen appears at the top of the can. If a customer didn't have a baby, the Mennen people pointed out that the contents made an "excellent tooth powder" and a delightful after shaving powder.

Cat. No.	Description	Dimensions	F	G	Ex
AP-6	Lyman's Cough Drops	23 x 28	100.00	600.00	1000.00
AP-7	Mennen's Talcum	6.5 x 12	25.00	45.00	75.00

NYAL
Nyal Company

ROYAL
The Merrill Co. Limited

All the talcs have their tops completely lithographed, usually with the company's monogram.

Cat. No.	Description	Dimensions	F	G	Ex
AP-8	Nyal Talcum	6.5 x 12.5	35.00	75.00	150.00
AP-9	Royal Talcum	6.5 x 12.5	100.00	250.00	500.00

Cabinets

The most colourful of the country store items appeared between 1885 and 1915, at the end of the Victorian and beginning of the Edwardian eras. If any period of time has characteristic attitudes, then these were years of optimism, richness of life and colour. This was a time, too, when children were positively doted upon.

ANCHOR SPOOL COTTON
Clark & Co.

BRAINERD & ARMSTRONG
Brainerd & Armstrong Co.

The ruby red glass inserts with contrasting white porcelain knobs make the Clark & Co. cabinet an important one in any collection.

This oak cabinet is unique because of the glass top allowing the purchaser to view the material without opening the drawer.

Cat. No.	Description	Dimensions	F	G	Ex
C-1	Anchor Spool Cotton	55 x 24 x 37	250.00	500.00	750.00
C-2	Brainerd & Armstrong	53 x 20 x 40	150.00	300.00	400.00

CORTICELLI
Corticelli Silk Co.

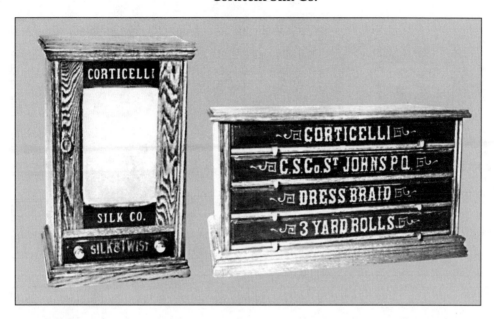

The Corticelli Silk Co. was located in St. Johns, Quebec, and used the motto: "Best in the World." The taller cabinet would have been placed on a counter top so that fashionable customers could see the effect of the materials they were choosing in the mirror.

As a rough rule of thumb, the more drawers a cabinet has, the greater its value. As well, a cabinet with stencilling on wooden drawer fronts is more valuable than one with stencilled glass drawer fronts, but not as valuable as one with ruby-red etched glass fronts.

Cat. No.	Description	Dimensions	F	G	Ex
C-3	Corticelli	38 x 60 x 33	200.00	350.00	500.00
C-4	Corticelli	60 x 34 x 40	150.00	300.00	500.00

"THE AGES OF WOMEN"
Diamond Dye Company
"THE BALLOON"

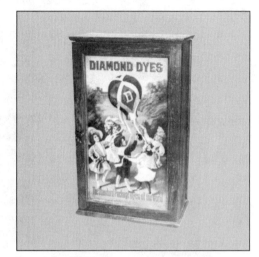

The Diamond Dye cabinets epitomize the age.

Rich in detail, in life and colour, the best of them featured beautiful children in gaily coloured clothes.

Cat. No.	Description	Dimensions	F	G	Ex
C-5	"The Ages of Women"	58 x 77 x 26	350.00	650.00	1000.00
C-6	"The Balloon"	41 x 63 x 21	350.00	650.00	1000.00

"THE GOVERNESS"   "THE MANSION"
Diamond Dye Company

   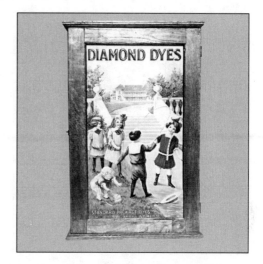

This cabinet is one of the most attractive large units. It bears a 1906 copyright by Wells Richardson Co. for both Canada and the United States.

"The Mansion" is one of three small cabinets, and is the most colourful of all. When full the cabinets held forty-eight different colours of dye in packets that sold for 10 cents each.

Cat. No.	Description	Dimensions	F	G	Ex
C-7	"The Governess"	58 x 77 x 26	500.00	1000.00	5000.00
C-8	"The Mansion"	41 x 63 x 21	350.00	650.00	1000.00

DR. DANIELS'   JACQUOT'S

For agreeing to stock Dr. Daniels' products, the store proprietor was given this stunning cabinet. A common American version lists all the products on the door, which greatly detracts from the graphic impact of the lithographed front. Dr. Daniels put his portrait on all his products.

An older style cabinet.

Cat. No.	Description	Dimensions	F	G	Ex
C-9	Dr. Daniels'	54.5 x 73.5 x 19	600.00	1200.00	1800.00
C-10	Jacquot's	32.5 x 53 x 32	100.00	175.00	250.00

Calendars

COCA-COLA
Coca-Cola Ltd.

F.X. GOSSELIN
F.X. Gosselin

Giveaways such as calendars have been a part of advertising from its beginning. Out of the thousands that have been produced, one of the prettiest is shown: an early Coke calendar. Because Coca-Cola is a specialized collecting category, the price of the beautiful pre-1925 Coke calendars has soared.

Pretty girls have always been a popular feature of calendars.

Cat. No.	Description	Dimensions	F	G	Ex
CAL-1	Coca-Cola	39.5 x 89.5	250.00	700.00	1000.00
CAL-2	F.X. Gosselin	30 x 41	25.00	60.00	100.00

HOOD'S SARSPARILLA
C.I. Hood & Co.

JACK'S GENERAL STORE
J. Nepon

The Hood's Sarsaparilla calendar for 1895 is the Canadian version with a special message from C.I. Hood himself "to the people of Canada." On the back, "especially calculated for C.I. Hood and Co." are the 1895 Astronomical Events for Canada, featuring five eclipses.

Cat. No.	Description	Dimensions	F	G	Ex
CAL-3	Hood's	12 x 19.5	30.00	60.00	125.00
CAL-4	Jack's General Store	29 x 52	25.00	50.00	75.00

METROPOLITAN
Metropolitan Life Insurance Company

Cat. No.	Description	Dimensions	F	G	Ex
CAL-5	Metropolitan	26 x 43	20.00	40.00	60.00

Clocks (Promotional)

AUGUST FLOWER

BLACK CAT
Nonsuch Mfg. Co. Limited

This clock is still a one-of-a-kind item. The design is painted on the reverse of the glass face.

This Black Cat clock is a great country store item, probably the best piece of Canadian antique advertising in existence. The lithographed front is nailed onto a wooden frame and the clock is operated by a simple alarm-clock sized unit. The clock dates from 1898; the tin front was made by the Macdonald Mfg. Co. Ltd. of Toronto. The clock is admired for its excellent graphics, the strong use of vivid colour, and because the clock form is extremely desirable.

Cat. No.	Description	Dimensions	F	G	Ex
CL-1	August Flower Clock	30.5 x 30.5	250.00	500.00	750.00
CL-2	Black Cat Clock	45 x 60	3000.00	7500.00	15000.00+

L.O. GROTHE
L.O. Grothe Company

This clock stand helped to resolve an antique puzzle. The Boston Cigar mirror (M-6) was thought to be Canadian because three had been found in Quebec and Ontario. Similarly, Peg-Top Cigar advertising abounds in Canada. Were these companies therefore Canadian? The discovery of this clock stand from the L.O. Grothe Co. of Montreal proves both products to be Canadian, and from Montreal. Intended to hold a small clock, the piece is cast iron and weighs ten pounds. it was produced by the Acme Litho Company.

In the 1990s recasts of this item have appeared, with rougher casting and no trace of original finish. The original clock should be marked L.O. Grothe.

Cat. No.	Description	Dimensions	F	G	Ex
CL-3	Grothe Clock Stand	41 x 29	125.00	350.00	750.00

Coffee Mills

Coffee mills are the universal symbol of the country store. They attract people who don't own one antique item, and they still fascinate the advanced collector. There are many sizes and brand names, all American. There were no coffee mills made in Canada. Coffee mills that retain original stencilling and drawer are much more desirable than those with replaced parts or restored finish. The term "coffee mill" refers to those used in stores. A "coffee grinder" is the name for the little machine used in homes.

COLES
Coles Mfg. Co.

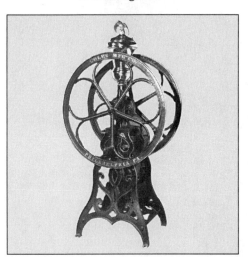

ELGIN
Elgin National

Probably the most spectacular mill in Canada! As tall as a man, this Coles Mfg. Co. mill from Philadelphia still has its original coat of paint with the stencilling and the gold leaf on the front of the original hopper. It was the mill that served the small town of Markdale, Ontario, and it is the largest size ever made.

The Elgin was made by Woodruff and Edwards of Elgin, Illinois.

Cat. No.	Description	Dimensions	F	G	Ex
CM-1	Coles	91 wheel diameter x 179	700.00	1500.00	2500.00
CM-2	Elgin National	43 wheel diameter x 71	300.00	500.00	800.00

ENTERPRISE
Enterprise Manufacturing Co.

SWIFT
Swift Mill

This particular mill, one of the smallest, is popular because it can fit nicely into a modern kitchen.

The Swift mill comes from the Lane Brothers, Poughkeepsie, N.Y.

Cat. No.	Description	Dimensions	F	G	Ex
CM-3	Enterprise	22 wheel diameter x 38	300.00	600.00	800.00
CM-4	Swift	30 wheel diameter x 45	300.00	500.00	800.00

Coffee Tins

Coffee was at first shipped as green beans, and householders would roast, grind, and blend their own. Around 1800, importers began to ship roasted beans in tin containers, and to provide small take-home canisters for the retailer, who would grind and blend to order right in the store, and then fill the canister for the purchaser. Eventually, importers began to do the whole process themselves — roasting, grinding, and blending.

Thus, sizes of coffee and tea tins include large store bins and smaller canisters which the retailer would fill for the customer to take home. Both might have been labelled with the importer's name. By the early twentieth century importers began to pre-package their teas and coffees in ready-to-buy small tins, and the store bins fell out of use.

In coffee and tea tins, top quality is still desired by collectors, but lesser quality tins sell well to decorators because of size, colour, and graphics.

BEE

The 1-lb. size coffee tin is very collectable in the United States. This one has a paper label with a bee motif that is unusual for a coffee tin. Just about any animal design on a tin makes it collectable.

Cat. No.	Description	Dimensions	F	G	Ex
CT-1	Bee Coffee	10 x 14	25.00	40.00	70.00

BRAID'S GOLDSWORTH
W. Braid & Co.

Different views of Vancouver are found on the back of the Braid tin.

The 1-lb. canister was a popular item, and was apparently designed as a souvenir item.

Cat. No.	Description	Dimensions	F	G	Ex
CT-2	Braid's Goldsworth Coffee	10.5 x 17	75.00	250.00	400.00

BRITANNIA

GREIG'S WHITE SWAN
The Robert Greig Co. Limited

This store bin illustrates the Canadian fascination with the Empire and the monarchy. Edward VII had toured North America as a young man, and the popularity he gained then never left him.The tin has a striking royal purple background.

The swan trademark makes this tin attractive to those who collect animal or bird themes.

Cat. No.	Description	Dimensions	F	G	Ex
CT-3	Britannia Coffee	34.5 x 50 x 34	150.00	400.00	600.00
CT-4	Greig's White Swan Coffee	12.5 x 11 x 9	20.00	35.00	50.00

KEARNEY BROS.
Kearney Bros. Limited

KING COLE
T.H. Estabrook Co. Ltd.

The Chateau Frontenac canister is another that would serve as a souvenir of Canada.

The highly-coloured 1 lb. King Cole is very collectable because of its attractive illustration. It comes from St. John, N.B., post 1930.

Cat. No.	Description	Dimensions	F	G	Ex
CT-5	Kearney Brothers Frontenac Coffee	10.5 x 17	25.00	50.00	85.00
CT-6	King Cole Coffee	10.5 x 15	50.00	125.00	200.00

| **LADIES DELIGHT** | **LADIES DELIGHT** |
| McLarens Limited | McLarens Limited |

The MacLaren's 60-lb. store bin is exceptional on several counts. It and the Todhunter (CT-11) are the only ones known to have the curved slant lift top. Store bins this size are a rarity and the excellent condition of this one is unusual. The colours are vivid and the picture-within-a-picture adds to the fascination of the tin. The smaller label declares that "this coffee is cleaned and roasted by the most recently-invented machinery."

This tin is a companion to the 60-lb. bin. The graphics on the bin were also used on the tin.

Cat. No.	Description	Dimensions	F	G	Ex
CT-7	McLarens Ladies Delight Bin	38.5 x 69 x 35	200.00	650.00	1000.00
CT-8	McLarens Ladies Delight Coffee	30 x 42.5	125.00	300.00	500.00

PRIDE OF ARABIA

RODEO
T.H. Estabrook Co. Ltd.

Key wind coffees (those opened with a small key provided with the tin) is a category growing in popularity. They are usually from the 1940s and 1950s. Shown are the 1/2-lb. and 1-lb. sizes.

Very rare, with the price reflecting the strong western interest in tin collecting

Cat. No.	Description	Dimensions	F	G	Ex
CT-9	Pride of Arabia Coffee	Various sizes	15.00	25.00	50.00
CT-10	Rodeo Coffee	19.2 x 20.5	100.00	500.00	1000.00+

TODHUNTER'S EXCELSIOR
Todhunter & Mitchell Co.

TRADE MILLS
Trade Mills Coffee & Spices

The Todhunter bin is, so far, the only one of its kind known. The monogram stands for Todhunter & Mitchell, a Toronto company. The label depicts a tin that has never been found, Excelsior Coffee. The condition of this bin is not as fine as it might be, but for a store bin it's considered superb. Store bins took a lot of bumping since they were designed to be floor display pieces. Notice also the Todhunter's advertising mirror that appears in the "Mirror" chapter.

The Trade Mills tin has a paper label that is not quite the right size glued onto it. We know it's Canadian only because of the existence of a canning jar embossed "Trade Mills Coffee & Spices - Montreal."

Cat. No.	Description	Dimensions	F	G	Ex
CT-11	Todhunter's Excelsior Coffee	38.5 x 69 x 35	200.00	650.00	1000.00
CT-12	Trade Mills Coffee	17 x 23 x 17	25.00	50.00	85.00

WHEAT SHEAF
Codville & Co. and
Gold Standard Manfg. Co.

Very collectable, these canisters have the same brand name and are from the same city, but were made for different companies. They both have a strong western Canadian identity, with Prairie harvest scenes, and one fairly dripping with maple leaves.

Cat. No.	Description	Dimensions	F	G	Ex
CT-13	Wheat Sheaf Coffee (Codville)	10.8 x 19	75.00	225.00	350.00
CT-14	Wheat Sheaf Coffee (Gold Standard)	10.6 x 19	100.00	350.00	700.00

Comestibles

CAVERLY & HORTON LARD
Caverly & Horton

Lard pails abounded in an era when every housewife made her own pie crust. The pig, from which lard comes, is a common motif on lard pails, as seen here on an Aylmer firm's tin.

Cat. No.	Description	Dimensions	F	G	Ex
COM-1	Caverly & Horton	14 x 14.5	25.00	50.00	75.00

BISCUIT TINS
Christie, Brown & Co. Limited

BISCUIT TINS
Christie, Brown & Co. Limited

An 1874-1902 commemorative tin.

A gift tin of biscuits for men of the Canadian Expeditionary Force fighting in France and Belgium during World War I, 1914-1918.

Cat. No.	Description	Dimensions	F	G	Ex
COM-2	Christie Brown	22 x 22 x 7	90.00	200.00	300.00
COM-3	Christie Brown	22 x 14 x 7	20.00	30.00	45.00

BISCUIT TIN
Christie, Brown & Co. Limited

The roof of this delightful truck opens up to reveal the cookies inside. Probably a special packaging for the Christmas trade, a tin similar to this was issued by the Perrin's Biscuit Company. Despite the Toronto, Montreal and Quebec addresses, the truck was probably made in England since the steering wheel is on the right hand side and the licence plate reads AL 4107. Tins that were made to be used later as toys are very collectable, since they are desired equally as much by toy and tin collectors.

Cat. No.	Description	Dimensions	F	G	Ex
COM-4	Christie Brown Truck	25 x 13.5 x 10	350.00	750.00	1000.00+

CIRCUS CLUB MALLOWS
Harry Horne Company Ltd.

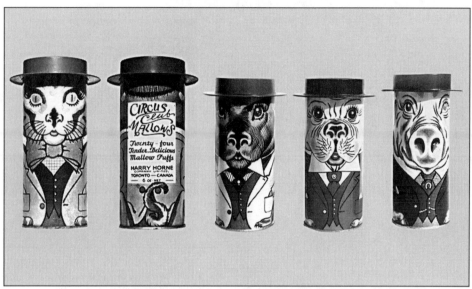

From left to right: Cat, Rear view cat, unknown, dog, pig

There are no tin manufacturer's markings on the Harry Horne brand tin, but the brand was very popular in the 1930s. There are six cartooned animal tins to collect, the cat being the most common. Other animals in the series include the monkey, the elephant, the dog, and the pig, all in full colour.

Cat. No.	Description	Dimensions	F	G	Ex
COM-5	Cat	10.5 across hat x 18	60.00	100.00	200.00
COM-6	What Is It?	10.5 across hat x 18	60.00	150.00	250.00
COM-7	Dog	10.5 across hat x 18	60.00	150.00	250.00
COM-8	Pig	10.5 across hat x 18	60.00	150.00	250.00
COM-9	Elephant (not shown)	10.5 across hat x 18	60.00	150.00	250.00
COM-10	Monkey (not shown)	10.5 across hat x 18	60.00	150.00	250.00

CORONA

Chewing gum tins are very collectable.

COWAN'S

The Cowan's tin is unusual because it features a pretty lady on all four sides of the tin.

Cat. No.	Description	Dimensions	F	G	Ex
COM-11	Corona Chewing Gum	8 x 2.5	30.00	75.00	125.00
COM-12	Cowan's Cocoa	24 x 27.5	40.00	90.00	150.00

DOUKHOBOR
Christian Community of Universal Brotherhood

ENGLISH TOMS
Crother's Confectionary

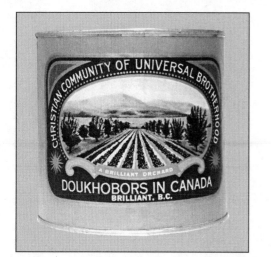

In general tins with paper labels are not nearly as collectable as those with the designs lithographed right on the tin. However, the historical interest of the Doukhobor tin makes it desirable to most collectors. The Christian Community of Universal Brotherhood purchased the Kootenay Jam Factory in Nelson, B.C. in 1911 and in 1915 relocated the factory to Brilliant, B.C.

Cat. No.	Description	Dimensions	F	G	Ex
COM-13	Doukhobor Household Jam	13 x 12.2	10.00	25.00	40.00
COM-14	English Toms	16.5 x 24.5	30.00	70.00	125.00

LARD
F.W. Fearman Co.

GUNNS MAPLE LEAF
Gunns Limited

Cat. No.	Description	Dimensions	F	G	Ex
COM-15	Fearman Lard	14 x 14.5	25.00	50.00	75.00
COM-16	Gunns Maple Leaf Lard	13 x 13.5	25.00	50.00	75.00

LONDON PEARL
Todhunter Mitchell Co.

Todhunter Mitchell cocoa bean bin.

Cat. No.	Description	Dimensions	F	G	Ex
COM-17	London Pearl Cocoa	22.5 x 25	40.00	90.00	150.00

PERRIN'S CANDY
Perrin's Biscuit and Confectionary Co.

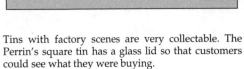

Tins with factory scenes are very collectable. The Perrin's square tin has a glass lid so that customers could see what they were buying.

These giant candy pails are very sturdy and for extra strength are ridged all around. They were apparently used for shipping, since the Perrin's pail has a label reading, "This package is for E. Scott and Son, Niagara Falls, Ontario via truck."

Cat. No.	Description	Dimensions	F	G	Ex
COM-18	Perrin's Candy —Tin	17 x 14	25.00	35.00	60.00
COM-19	Perrin's Candy — Pail	26 x 23.5	25.00	60.00	100.00

ROBERTSON'S
Robertson Bros. Ltd.

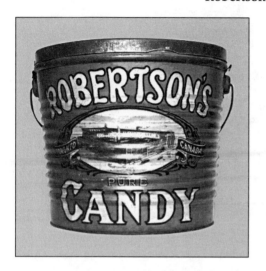

Front view

In general, candy, cough drop and gum country store items are highly sought after. There seemed to be very few good Canadian candy tins until this rare item came along.

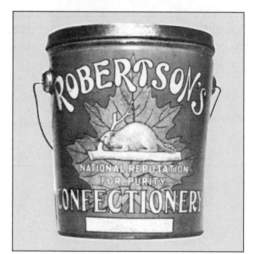

Rear view

Cat. No.	Description	Dimensions	F	G	Ex
COM-20	Robertson's Candy	26 x 23.5	35.00	90.00	150.00
COM-21	Robertson's Confectionery	14 base x 18	50.00	150.00	350.00

SWEET BRIER LARD
W. Wight & Co.

The Sweet Brier lard came in a variety of sizes. This is the 3-lb. size.

Cat. No.	Description	Dimensions	F	G	Ex
COM-22	Sweet Brier Lard	13 x 13.5	25.00	50.00	75.00

TILLSON'S PAN DRIED OATS
Tillson

WATKINS BAKING POWDER
Watkins

This tin is also eagerly sought by toy bank collectors. The charming Tillson's Oats giveaway bank bears this inscription on the back:

> Maw says to save my pennies for
> a future rainy day.
> But if it never never rains
> I'll save 'em anyway.
> And when I am a wealthy man
> I'll marry Effie Coates,
> and feed my children every day
> On Tillson's Pan Dried Oats.

Cat. No.	Description	Dimensions	F	G	Ex
COM-23	Tillson's Oats	6.5 x 9.6	75.00	200.00	300.00
COM-24	Watkins Baking Powder	8 x 13.5	10.00	20.00	30.00

Dispensers and Displays

Dispensers were the front line in a company's attack on a customer. They would confront him at point of purchase, which is why a lot of money went into producing them. The results were the most imaginative, colourful, distinctly-shaped pieces found in Canadian country stores. Some of the product names are familiar: Wrigley's, Hires, Planters, while others, such as Mexican Fruit Gum and the Sun Garter, didn't last. Except for coffee mills, nothing so thoroughly represents the old-time country store as its dispensers.

BACHELOR CIGAR DISPENSER
Wilsons

CHOCOLATE DISPLAY CASE
Cadbury Schweppes

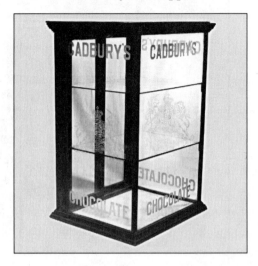

Probably the most colourful of all the Canadian cigar dispensers, the Bachelor proclaims itself "Canada's National Smoke." The machine was made by the Fisher Motor Company, and extra colour was added with the reverse-on-glass windows at the top of the unit. This dispenser was designed to hold packs of five cigars, and was on loan to the store.

Display cases for country stores came in all sizes and shapes, although very few Canadian ones have advertising etched in the glass. The Cadbury's case is possibly English. Cadbury's is English, and the dozens of cases that have been found in Canada could have come over as part of container loads of English antiques.

Cat. No.	Description	Dimensions	F	G	Ex
D-1	Bachelor	27 x 32 x 26	100.00	200.00	350.00
D-2	Cadbury's Showcase	37 x 60 x 32	125.00	200.00	300.00

GLASS CANDY JARS
Dominion Glass Company

HIRES SYRUP DISPENSERS
Charles E. Hires Company

Candy display jars such as these are thought to be made by the Dominion Glass Company of Canada because of the familiar pattern on the neck and lid of the jars.

All old syrup dispensers for soft drinks seem to be attractively made. This hour-glass Hires is a good example. The bottom inscription reads: "Loaned by and the property, The Charles E. Hires Company, Toronto. Made in the United States."

Cat. No.	Description	Dimensions	F	G	Ex
D-3	Glass Candy Jars	various sizes		Range — 75.00 - 300.00	
D-4	Hires	20 x 36 x 20	200.00	350.00	500.00

GLASS COUGH DROP JAR
Lutted's

MAGIC BAKING POWDER
W.Gillett Company

The Lutted's jar may well be American in origin, but it was found in the basement of an old Canadian country store. The lids to these jars do not always fit properly as they were made separately and simply added later.

The Magic Baking Powder tins are all wired together to form a display piece for a general store. The W. Gillett company first issued these tins. Today Standard Brands still uses similar graphics.

Cat. No.	Description	Dimensions	F	G	Ex
D-5	Lutted's Cough Drops	14.5 diameter x 27	150.00	250.00	400.00
D-6	Magic Baking Powder Tins	15 x 83	70.00	150.00	250.00

MEXICAN GUM DISPENSER
London Novelty Company

O-PEE-CHEE GUM DISPENSER
O-Pee-Chee Co.

Detail of coin slots

The Mexican Gum machine was made by the Enamelled Steel Sign Company, Chicago, and was on loan to stores from the London Novelty Company. This machine would accept only the large pennies.

This O-Pee-Chee machine was adapted for use with both large and small Canadian pennies. There is no manufacturer's mark.

Cat. No.	Description	Dimensions	F	G	Ex
D-7	Mexican Gum	16 x 69 x 16	500.00	1000.00	1500.00
D-8	O-Pee-Chee Gum	22 x 116 x 21	500.00	1000.00	1500.00

PLANTER'S BARREL JAR
Planters Nut & Chocolate Co. Ltd.

PLANTER'S 8-SIDED JAR
Planters Nut & Chocolate Co. Ltd.

The barrel jar comes with a paper decal and silver paint on the two Mr. Peanuts.

The eight-sided 5-cent jar has been reproduced and this has drastically reduced the desirability of the authentic one.

Cat. No.	Description	Dimensions	F	G	Ex
D-9	Planters Barrel Jar	20.5 diameter x 30.5	150.00	250.00	350.00
D-10	Planters 8-sided Jar	20.3 x 26.1 x 20.3	60.00	100.00	150.00

Note: The Planters Peanut Company began business in 1906 at Wilkes-Barre, Pennsylvania. In 1916 a fourteen-year-old boy submitted his sketch of P. Peanut — commonly called Mister — as a symbol for the prospering company. An artist added a monocle and a bent leg, and one of the most easily-recognized trade marks of our time was born. Most Planters promotional items were used in Canada as well as the United States.

PLANTER'S CORNER JAR
Planters Nut & Chocolate Co. Ltd.

POST CARD RACK

The jar with a peanut moulded into each corner was the hardest to produce, but it is much more common in Canada than in the United States.

The post card rack in a general store was usually the swivel type, but here a wall version does the job. The rage for collecting post cards has made these racks impossible to find.

Cat. No.	Description	Dimensions	F	G	Ex
D-11	Planters 4-Peanut Corner Jar	19.5 x 33 x 19.5	100.00	175.00	250.00
D-12	Post Card Rack	14 x 87	25.00	40.00	60.00

THE SUN GARTER DISPLAY

The garter is supposed to be holding up a stocking on a male leg. The display case, which dates from 1905, came free with an order for three dozen pairs of garters.

Cat. No.	Description	Dimensions	F	G	Ex
D-13	The Sun Garter	19 x 27.5 x 16.5	100.00	175.00	250.00

TUCKETTS CIGARS
The Tuckett Tobacco Company

TUCKETTS CIGARS & TOBACCO
The Tuckett Tobacco Company

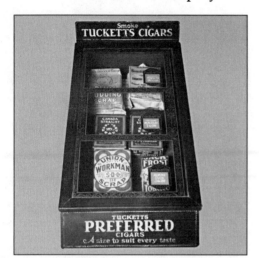

The Tuckett Tobacco Company issued at least half a dozen different dispensers, all in a maroon, gold and black colour scheme. The Fisher Motor Co. or General Steel Wares between them seem to have made most of the dispensers in Canada. Fisher made everything for Tuckett, who was one of the more successful tobacco magnates. He started out by stock-piling tobacco behind American Civil War battle lines, waiting for the battle to pass him by, and ended up as Mayor of Hamilton, Ontario.

Cat. No.	Description	Dimensions	F	G	Ex
D-14	Tucketts Cigars	28.5 x 28.5 x 50	60.00	125.00	200.00
D-15	Tucketts Cigars & Tobaccos	44 X 18.5 X 20	60.00	125.00	200.00

TUCKETTS PLUG TOBACCO
The Tuckett Tobacco Company

 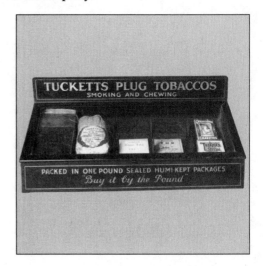

Cat. No.	Description	Dimensions	F	G	Ex
D-16	Tucketts Plug Tobaccos	17 x 17 x 21	60.00	125.00	200.00
D-17	Tucketts Plug Tobaccos	47 x 30 x 48	60.00	125.00	200.00

WRIGLEY'S
Wm. Wrigley Company

   This dispenser was introduced circa 1915, the year the "Sprightly Spearman" was introduced. Both dispensers are distinctly Canadian and very rare. The gum is not original. The square dispenser, made by the Fisher Motor Co., successor to the Tudhope Company of Orillia, is a bit newer than the round one. Wrigley's has always spent a lot of money advertising. Wm. Wrigley was once asked why he continued to advertise so much when he already had such a large share of the market. Mr. Wrigley motioned to the aircraft he was in at the time and asked why he shouldn't tell the pilot to shut off his engine since the plane was going along nicely and was quite high up.

Cat. No.	Description	Dimensions	F	G	Ex
D-18	Wrigley's Round	34 x 33 x 16	300.00	600.00	1000.00
D-19	Wrigley's Square	33.5 x 51.5 x 16	300.00	600.00	1000.00

General Store Fixtures

COMFORT SOAP STOOL
Pugsley Dingman Company

CORTICELLI TABLE
Corticelli Silk Company

The Comfort Soap stool is one of the many give-aways the company offered regular users of its product. It came in a couple of styles, both very sturdy.

The table is a very interesting piece for a number of reasons. The legs screw off easily, perhaps to make it easier for salesmen to deliver them as they made their calls. The table also opens up as if it were a writing desk. It may have been meant to hold sales goods, but it is only 6 cm deep. It doesn't have a tape measure along one side to make it more functional, and its purpose in a country store is a bit of a mystery.

Cat. No.	Description	Dimensions	F	G	Ex
GS-1	Comfort Soap Stool	35 base x 55	35.00	75.00	150.00
GS-2	Corticelli Table	Top 91 x 45.5, 69 height	35.00	75.00	150.00

SCALES
Gurney & Ware Co.

DRUGGIST'S TRUNK
Lyman Bros.

The advertising on the marble makes these otherwise
plain scales very attractive. The Gurney & Ware Co.
was a large scale manufacturer located in Hamilton,
Ontario.

Cat. No.	Description	Dimensions	F	G	Ex
GS-3	Gurney & Ware Scales	49 x 18	125.00	200.00	250.00
GS-4	Lyman Bros. Trunk	80 x 49 x 54	40.00	75.00	125.00

PLANTERS SCOOP
Planters Nut & Chocolate Company

BROOM RACK
T.S. Simms & Co. Ltd

The Planters tin scoop would measure 5 cents worth of peanuts to go into a nickel glassine bag.

This wooden broom rack was furnished by the T.S. Simms Co. of St. John, New Brunswick.

Cat. No.	Description	Dimensions	F	G	Ex
GS-5	Planters Scoop	4.5 top x 7	40.00	60.00	100.00
GS-6	Broom Rack	33.5 x 34		Rare	

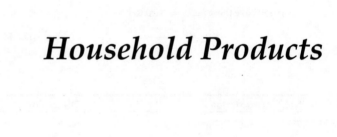

Household Products

COMFORT SOAP RAG DOLL
Pugsley Dingman Company

CRYSTAL GLOSS
Imperial Starch Co. Limited

Rag dolls like these are now hard to find.

If the Macdonald Company designed a beautiful tin, its turn of the century arch-rival, the Thomas Davidson Company, would design a tin just as attractive for a competing brand. Here Davidson did a stunning full-colour lithograph for the Imperial Starch Co. on a tin with an unusual shape.

Cat. No.	Description	Dimensions	F	G	Ex
HHP-1	Comfort Soap Rag Doll	68 tall	60.00	125.00	200.00
HHP-2	Crystal Gloss Starch	20 x 20	75.00	150.00	350.00

GANTZ INSECT POWDER
Gantz

KLEANALL AUTO BODY POLISH
Domestic Specialty Company

Anything could, and did, come in tins, from insect powder to chewing gum and even record needles.

The Kleanall tin has a paper label

Cat. No.	Description	Dimensions	F	G	Ex
HHP-3	Gantz Insect Powder	5 x 8.5	10.00	25.00	40.00
HHP-4	Kleanall Auto Polish	7.5 x 14	25.00	50.00	75.00

LILY WHITE STARCH
Brantford Starch Co. Ltd

John Sebert, the dean of Canadian tin collectors, has stated that this tin shows "perhaps the most outstanding example of lithography done by the Macdonald firm." The tin bears the inscription, "Design Registered 1895."

Cat. No.	Description	Dimensions	F	G	Ex
HHP-5	Lily White Starch	15.5 x 28.5	50.00	175.00	350.00

NEEDLE TINS
Various Manufacturers

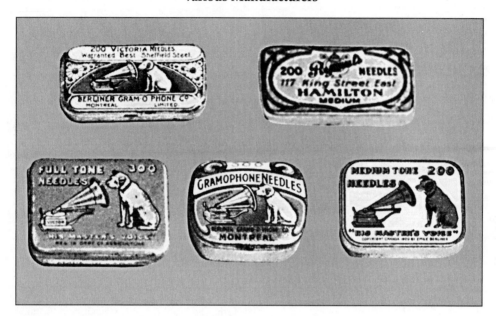

Cat. No.	Description	Dimensions	F	G	Ex
HHP-6	Needle Tin	5 x 2.5	15.00	25.00	35.00
HHP-7	Needle Tin	5 x 2.5	15.00	20.00	25.00
HHP-8	Needle Tin	4 x 3	15.00	25.00	40.00
HHP-9	Needle Tin	3.5 x 3	15.00	20.00	25.00
HHP-10	Needle Tin	4 x 3	15.00	25.00	40.00

SHINO STOVE POLISH
E. Hawes & Co. Limited

SILVER GLOSS STARCH
The Canada Starch Co. Limited

The horseshoe shape label is an unusual one attempted only on starch tins by the Thos. Davidson firm. The beautiful embossed design and unusual shape complement a product that won eight medals at industrial fairs, including the Agricultural and Industrial Exhibition for the Province of Quebec, and the Industrial Exhibition Association of Toronto.

Cat. No.	Description	Dimensions	F	G	Ex
HHP-11	Shino Stove Polish	8 x 5.3	15.00	25.00	40.00
HHP-12	Silver Gloss Starch	15.5 x 21	35.00	75.00	150.00

SURPRISE SOAP STRING DISPENSER

SURPRISE SOAP DOLL

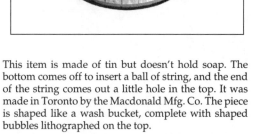

This item is made of tin but doesn't hold soap. The bottom comes off to insert a ball of string, and the end of the string comes out a little hole in the top. It was made in Toronto by the Macdonald Mfg. Co. The piece is shaped like a wash bucket, complete with shaped bubbles lithographed on the top.

Surprise Soap came from St. Stephen, N.B. The pumice soap is from the London Soap Company.

Cat. No.	Description	Dimensions	F	G	Ex
HHP-10	Surprise Soap String Holder	16.5 x 11	70.00	200.00	300.00
HHP-11	Soap Rag Dolls	68 tall	60.00	125.00	200.00

TIGER WHITE LEAD
The Steel Company of Canada Ltd.

Tins with birds or animals are highly collectable, whatever the contents. Few people collect old paint tins, but many collectors would be proud to own the full-colour Tiger White Lead.

Cat. No.	Description	Dimensions	F	G	Ex
HHP-12	Tiger White Lead	18 at top x 18	25.00	50.00	90.00

Mirrors (Promotional)

BOSTON CIGAR MIRROR

Cat. No.	Description	Dimensions	F	G	Ex
MIR-1	Boston Cigar Mirror	36 x 86	150.00	250.00	400.00

CORTICELLI MIRROR
Corticelli Silk Company

Cat. No.	Description	Dimensions	F	G	Ex
MIR- 2	Corticelli Mirror	100.5 x 63.5	150.00	250.00	400.00

TODHUNTER'S MIRROR
Todhunter & Mitchell Company

The Todhunter mirror, with its gold lettering, was given free to larger
country stores around 1905. Only a handful seem to have survived.

Cat. No.	Description	Dimensions	F	G	Ex
MIR -3	Todhunter's Coffee Mirror	167 x 60	350.00	600.00	1000.00

Paper

This section contains items made from paper, such as posters and labels, as well as all paper-under-glass products. Paper-under-glass is the name used to describe paper advertisements which were framed by the company whose product is advertised. The "pictures" would be hung in country stores to promote the product, and to decorate. The term has also come to mean any framed — and thus behind glass — advertising piece.

There are strict rules governing what is considered good paper-under-glass and what is inferior. The best pieces show the advertised product prominently, and come in a frame that is marked with the company name.

COMFORT SOAP   DINGMAN'S SOAP
Pugsley Dingman Co.

Cat. No.	Description	Dimensions	F	G	Ex
PAP-1	Comfort Soap	50 x 70	125.00	250.00	400.00
PAP-2	Dingman's Soap	50 x 73	125.00	250.00	400.00

Note: Both of these pieces are cut down to fit a new unmarked frame. They are attractive still because of the subject: children. A rule of thumb: beautiful women and charming children are as desirable in paper-under-glass as is a prominent picture of the product.

B. HOUDE & CO.

LABATT'S

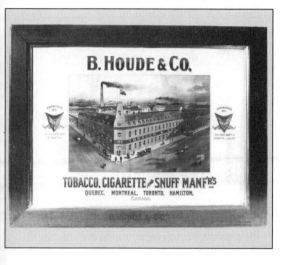

Even though the copy for this c. 1895 paper-under-glass mentions Montreal, Toronto and Hamilton, the company's tins are only marked Quebec City. The B. Houde Co. started in 1841 and was bought out by the American Tobacco Co. of Canada in 1903, ending the reign of Canada's largest tobacco company. Notice the marked frame on this piece.

While this piece shows the product prominently and comes in a marked frame, it just isn't rare enough to command more money.

Cat. No.	Description	Dimensions	F	G	Ex
PAP-3	B. Houde & Co.	101 x 78	400.00	600.00	1800.00
PAP-4	Labatt's	50.5 x 65	175.00	300.00	600.00

TUCKETTS
Geo. F. Tuckett & Son

The Victorians used "before and after" themes in advertising. The very young pipe smoker is pictured in the rich, dark colours of an old painting. The piece shown was reframed at some point, which reduces its value.

This Tucketts item is one of the better pieces of Canadian paper-under-glass. The product is displayed many times and the frame is marked. The family scene is quite interesting. Note the male members taking the prominent space, and the picture of the Tuckett factory in the background. This piece has been found in a different style of frame and also in canvas. It was produced circa 1895.

Cat. No.	Description	Dimensions	F	G	Ex
PAP-5	Before and After	82 x 66		Possibly unique	
PAP-6	Gathering	83 x 70	300.00	600.00	1000.00

PAPER LABELS

Many of the paper labels from old tin cans are works of art. Carefully framed they make excellent kitchen decor. This sampling of labels from Ontario produce cans has a distinctly western theme, probably because they are from the 1890 to 1910 period, when the opening of the Canadian west caught the imagination of the world.

Cat. No.	Description	Dimensions	F	G	Ex
PAP-7	Colonist Can Label	approx. 30 x 11	5.00	15.00	30.00
PAP-8	Golden West Can Label	approx. 30 x 11	5.00	15.00	30.00
PAP-9	Lasso Brand Can Label	approx. 30 x 11	5.00	15.00	30.00

PAPER POSTERS
Smithville Fair

The country store was a repository for posters of all kinds. Fairs were as popular then as now, and the local store was a place where everyone would see the announcement. The Smithville Fair put out an excellent poster each year and distributed them to local stores. Two criteria to look for in posters: a large picture and a distinct date.

Cat. No.	Description	Dimensions	F	G	Ex
PAP-10	Smithville Fair Poster	41 x 112	60.00	125.00	250.00

Peanut Butter Tins

For some reason, miniatures have always fascinated collectors. In tobacco tins it's the small ones, the "pocket" tins that are the most collectable. After these pocket tins, perhaps the next most collectable tins are the miniature peanut butter pails. Holding less than one pound, many were designed to appeal to children and to be used as pails in the sandbox after the peanut butter was eaten. The most desirable have cartoon scenes, patriotic themes or a picture of an animal.

BEAVER BRAND
Beaver Maple Products Limited

BOWES
Bowes Company Ltd.

Complete with maple leaves, the Beaver Brand tin is the favourite of many Canadian collectors.

Cat. No.	Description	Dimensions	F	G	Ex
PB-1	Beaver Brand	9.3 x 8.5	150.00	450.00	750.00
PB-2	Bowes	9.3 x 9.5	30.00	75.00	150.00

CLARK'S
W. Clark Limited

GOLD MEDAL
Gold Medal Products Limited

This pail enjoys terrific full-colour lithography, including the lid. The distinctly Canadian theme marks this pail as a great favourite.

Gold Medal Products packaged all its foodstuffs, such as coffee, baking powder and peanut butter in identically designed and colourful red, blue and gold tins.

Cat. No.	Description	Dimensions	F	G	Ex
PB-3	Clark's Scenes of Canada	8.6 x 8.7	100.00	250.00	400.00
PB-4	Gold Medal	7.6 x 9.5	20.00	40.00	60.00

JACK AND JILL
Loblaw Groceterias Co. Limited

A hard-to-find tin with a good theme, but the picture is small and there are only two colours (brown and gold).

Cat. No.	Description	Dimensions	F	G	Ex
PB-5	Jack and Jill	7.8 x 9	30.00	75.00	150.00

MACLAREN'S "TEA PARTY"
MacLaren-Wright Limited

The pleasantly drawn cartoon of two children playing "tea party" has made this tin very popular. In the background at the boy's feet is a peanut butter pail — a MacLaren's no doubt. An astonishing thing about the tin is the small size of the product name. Evidently the shape of the can defined the contents: peanut butter.

Cat. No.	Description	Dimensions	F	G	Ex
PB-6	MacLaren's Tea Party	7.9 x 9	30.00	75.00	150.00

MACLAREN'S
MacLaren-Wright Limited

Two cartoons on one pail — a real treat. The variation which has this picture on the back — the boy pulling the tin of MacLaren's peanut butter down on himself — is much rarer than the first version which bears only words on the other side.

This version of the MacLaren's tin has the slogan but no cartoon, much to the chagrin of collectors.

Cat. No.	Description	Dimensions	F	G	Ex
PB-7	MacLaren's Variation	7.9 x 9	150.00	400.00	700.00
PB-8	Maclaren's	7.6 x 9.5	20.00	40.00	60.00

OLD TYME
Canadian Maple Products Limited

PARROT
The Westport Company Limited

The Old Tyme is the most common Canadian peanut butter pail.

The Parrot tin is striking for its bold use of very fine colours.

Cat. No.	Description	Dimensions	F	G	Ex
PB-9	Old Tyme	8.7 x 8.9	20.00	35.00	50.00
PB-10	Parrot	7.5 x 8.6	350.00	1000.00	2000.00+

PETER RABBIT
Kelly Confection Co. Ltd.

Every inch of this tin is filled with detail in true Harrison Cady style. Now remembered mainly for his illustrations of Thornton Burgess' books about Peter Rabbit, Cady did more than 10,000 illustrations for magazines. A truly great tin because of the Peter Rabbit theme.

Cat. No.	Description	Dimensions	F	G	Ex
PB-11	Peter Rabbit	7.8 x 9.7	400.00	1000.00	2000.00+

SQUIRREL BRAND   SQUIRREL
The Canada Nut Co. Ltd.

Both tins are not properly peanut butter "pails" because they lack the little bail (handle), but their correct size keeps them in this collectable category.

Cat. No.	Description	Dimensions	F	G	Ex
PB-12	Squirrel	8.7 x 6.3	100.00	300.00	450.00
PB-13	Squirrel	7.8 x 9.6	30.00	75.00	125.00

SWEETHEART
IXL Spice and Coffee Mills

TEDDY BEAR
C. & J. Jones

Ever since Teddy Roosevelt refused to shoot a bear cub while on a hunting trip, the "Teddy" bear has been a symbol of innocence and childhood. A newspaper cartoonist recreated the scene, and the concept was seized by a toy manufacturer, who thought the public might respond to a cuddly toy named after the President. He obtained Roosevelt's permission to call it a "Teddy Bear" and sold every bear he could produce that year. The tin is stunning in its simplicity of design and the orange, blue and silver colour combination. It is very rare.

Cat. No.	Description	Dimensions	F	G	Ex
PB-14	Sweetheart	8.7 x 8.9	35.00	60.00	85.00
PB-15	Teddy Bear	9.2 x 8.8	250.00	700.00	1000.00

WHITE SWAN
White Swan Spices and Cereals Ltd.

Cat. No.	Description	Dimensions	F	G	Ex
PB-16	White Swan	7.8 x 8.9	50.00	125.00	200.00

Signs

There have been signs in country stores since the first merchant hung out a crudely-lettered piece of board that said "General Store." The earliest signs were made of wood, often carved in the shape of the product sold — for example, a boot — to help identify that product for the illiterate customer. Tin signs followed, then canvas and finally porcelain, cardboard and celluloid almost simultaneously in the 1900s.

There is a general rule of thumb about collecting Canadian country store signs. For signs of equal merit graphically, porcelain is better than tin, tin is better than celluloid, celluloid is better than cardboard, and there aren't enough canvas signs to worry about. Wooden signs are often regarded with suspicion because they are so easily and so often reproduced.

The porcelain signs in Margaret and Frank Williams' kitchen in 1979 are shown above. This picture in the 1979 edition caused more reaction than any other. People simply phoned up and said, "I want to do a wall like that one. Get me some porcelain signs." The result — a huge increase in prices. The 1979 price of the King Cole porcelain (on page 1070: $155. In 1996: $1000+.

ANTHONY FENCE
The Anthony Wire Fence Co. Limited

Anthony Fence is a tin sign made by Toledo Metal Sign Company, Toledo, Ohio

Cat. No.	Description	Dimensions	F	G	Ex
S-1	Anthony Fence tin	36 x 26	35.00	60.00	100.00

BULLDOG OVERALLS
Canada-Overall Co.

Cat. No.	Description	Dimensions	F	G	Ex
5-2	Bulldog Overalls framed tin	93 x 30	100.00	225.00	350.00

CANADA DRY

C.C.M. SERVICE
Canadian Cycle and Motor Company

Flange signs are designed to protrude from a wall.

Palm pushes (or presses) were placed on store doors to indicate where to push, and also to advertise the product. This push is tin; many others are porcelain.

Cat. No.	Description	Dimensions	F	G	E»
S-3	Canada Dry tin palm push	9 x 34	25.00	60.00	100.0
S-4	C.C.M. porcelain flange	41 x 31	200.00	450.00	700.0

COCA-COLA
Coca Cola Beverages Ltd.

DR. DANIELS'

Notice that the "trade mark reg." for the Coca-Cola sign is not inside the tail of the first C. That indicates the sign was made after 1940.

Dr. Daniels was an American concern that expanded into Canada. The company was prolific in its advertising and produced a magnificent tin-front cabinet (see C-9) as well as tins, advertising mirrors and other signs.

Cat. No.	Description	Dimensions	F	G	Ex
S-5	Coca-Cola	45 x 48.5	125.00	250.00	350.00
S-6	Dr. Daniels'	70 x 42	100.00	200.00	300.00

DIXIE'S CIGAR
Rock City Tobacco Co.

ELEPHANT WHITE LEAD
The Canada Paint Co. Limited

Complete with an easel-type stand at the back, the Elephant sign is made of "Enameloid" according to an inscription on the back, although it appears to be tin over cardboard. It appeared around 1915. Note the similarity between the paint tin pictured on this sign and the competition's "Tiger" brand tin pictured in the Household Goods chapter.

Cat. No.	Description	Dimensions	F	G	Ex
S-7	Dixie's Cigar tin over cardboard	36 x 26	200.00	500.00	1000.00
S-8	Elephant "enamaloid"	23.5 x 37.5	60.00	125.00	200.00

FIVE ROSES FLOUR	FROST'S
Pillsbury	

This porcelain palm push in vivid colour is one of the most beautiful found in Canada.

This sign, from the optical shop of the father of one of Ontario's most admired premiers, Leslie Frost, shows the art nouveau influence of the time.

Cat. No.	Description	Dimensions	F	G	Ex
S-9	Five Roses porcelain palm push	10.3 x 29.5	200.00	400.00	700.00
S-10	Frost's framed tin	78 x 58	125.00	225.00	350.00

M.S. GOSS

HIRES ROOT BEER
R.J. Hires Co.

Marked "Made in Canada."

Cat. No.	Description	Dimensions	F	G	Ex
S-11	M.S. Goss tin	40 x 25	60.00	125.00	200.0(
S-12	Hires tin palm push	10 x 36	25.00	60.00	100.0(

INDEPENDENT GROCER

KING COLE
T.H. Estabrook Co. Ltd.

The Macdonald Mfg. Co. of Toronto produced the powerful Independent Grocer sign. Could there be a better Canadian country store sign?

Cat. No.	Description	Dimensions	F	G	Ex
S-13	Independent Grocer tin	45.5 x 45.5	250.00	500.00	750.00
S-14	King Cole porcelain	23 x 38.5	250.00	750.00	1000.00+

KING COLE
T.H. Estabrook Co. Ltd.

Cat. No.	Description	Dimensions	F	G	Ex
S-15	King Cole porcelain palm push	7.6 x 28	50.00	100.00	150.00
S-16	King Cole porcelain door push	46 x 7.5	50.00	100.00	150.00

KUNTZ'S
Kuntz Company

LYONS'

The Kuntz company of Waterloo, Ontario produced some of the finest advertising beer trays known. However, the company didn't spend an equal effort on designing its signs.

Porcelain palm pushes are one of the most sought-after collectables. The Lyons' is the rarest in Canada, the Red Rose is the most common.

Cat. No.	Description	Dimensions	F	G	Ex
S-17	Kuntz's tin	71 x 50	40.00	75.00	125.00
S-18	Lyons' porcelain palm push	7.5 x 25	50.00	125.00	200.00

O'KEEFE'S
O'Keefe's Beverages Limited

These are over-sized tin signs intended for the outside of a building. Signs that picture the product are highly collectable.

Cat. No.	Description	Dimensions	F	G	Ex
S-19	O'Keefe's Lime Rickey tin	44 x 120	60.00	125.00	200.00
S-20	O'Keefe's Ginger Beer tin	150 x 92	60.00	125.00	200.00

OLD CHUM
Imperial Tobacco Company

OVERLAND

The Overland Triplex Springs sign is one of the few valuable Canadian cardboard signs.It is very collectable because of the circa 1930 car, the forerunner of today's Pontiacs.

Cat. No.	Description	Dimensions	F	G	Ex
S-21	Old Chum porcelain	77 x 46.5	60.00	125.00	250.00
S-22	Overland cardboard	85 x 39	100.00	200.00	300.00

PARKER'S DYE
Parker's Dye Works

PEG TOP
L.O. Grothe Ltd.

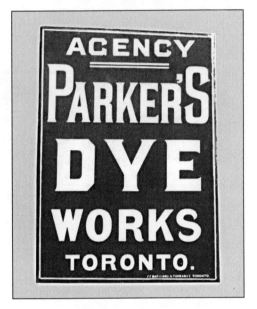

Cat. No.	Description	Dimensions	F	G	Ex
S-23	Parker's Dye porcelain	33 x 45	75.00	200.00	300.00
S-24	Peg Top porcelain	61 x 41	75.00	175.00	300.00

PEPSI-COLA

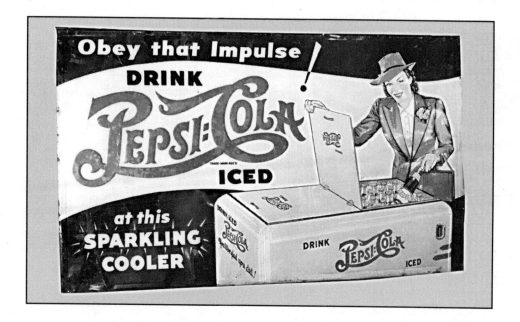

The pop cooler and the style of clothing date this sign as early 1940s. Pepsi-Cola made few signs as attractive as this one.

Cat. No.	Description	Dimensions	F	G	Ex
S-25	Pepsi-Cola tin	150 x 92	200.00	500.00	750.00

PILOT
Pilot Insurance Company

PURITY FLOUR

Cat. No.	Description	Dimensions	F	G	Ex
S-26	Pilot porcelain	46 x 31	50.00	125.00	175.00
S-27	Purity porcelain palm push	10.3 x 38.5	100.00	225.00	350.00

RED HAND
Somerville's

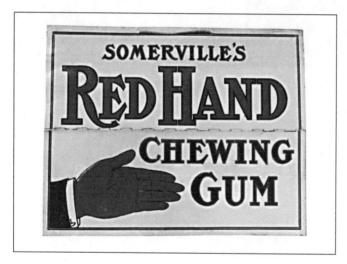

The second sign illustrated is hinged horizontally.

Cat. No.	Description	Dimensions	F	G	Ex
S-28	Red Hand tin	30 x 11.5	150.00	300.00	500.00
S-29	Red Hand hinged tin	40 x 31	100.00	225.00	400.00

RED ROSE TEA
T.H. Estabrook Co. Ltd.

RED ROSE TEA
T.H. Estabrook Co. Ltd.

Cat. No.	Description	Dimensions	F	G	Ex
S-30	Red Rose tin	29 x 44	30.00	50.00	75.00
S-31	Red Rose porcelain palm push	7.5 x 23.5	50.00	125.00	200.00

SALADA COFFEE
The Salada Tea Company

Salada made at least half a dozen different porcelain signs. This one is especially desirable because of its shape.

Cat. No.	Description	Dimensions	F	G	Ex
S-32	Salada Coffee porcelain	31 x 33	75.00	175.00	250.00

SALADA TEA
The Salada Tea Company

Cat. No.	Description	Dimensions	F	G	Ex
S-33	Salada porcelain door push	39 x 7.5	50.00	100.00	150.00
S-34	Salada porcelain door push	46 x 7.8	50.00	100.00	150.00

SALADA TEA
The Salada Tea Company

The advantage of porcelain over tin was that porcelain wouldn't rust or disintegrate in the wet, cold Canadian winters, and therefore porcelain signs are used much more frequently in Canada than in countries with a milder climate. The Salada Tea Company produced many porcelain signs and a whole variety of "boxes." Shown are the brown and the red in different sizes. They are prized for their shape and bright colours.

Cat. No.	Description	Dimensions	F	G	Ex
S-35	Salada Tea Box porcelain (brown)	32.5 x 13.5	75.00	175.00	250.00
S-36	Salada Tea Box porcelain (red)	38 x 17	75.00	175.00	250.00

SALADA
The Salada Tea Company

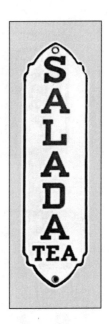

Cat. No.	Description	Dimensions	F	G	Ex
S-37	Salada Tea Pot porcelain	30 x 21	150.00	350.00	500.00
S-38	Salada porcelain palm push	6.5 x 24.5	50.00	125.00	200.00

SHELL MOTOR OIL
Shell Oil Company of Canada Ltd.

Shell oil used to come in tall glass bottles. This sign featuring the bottle is highly sought after by automotive collectors.

Cat. No.	Description	Dimensions	F	G	Ex
S-39	Shell Oil tin	49 x 155	100.00	200.00	300.00

SHERWIN-WILLIAMS PAINTS

Front   Back

This is a flange sign with a different image on each side.

Cat. No.	Description	Dimensions	F	G	Ex
S-40	Sherwin-Williams porcelain flange	56 x 41	75.00	150.00	250.00

SUNLIGHT SOAP
Lever Bros. Ltd.

TUCKETTS
The Tuckett Tobacco Company

This is one of the few canvas signs found in Canada. The French on this sign tells us it was used in Quebec. The sign is a full-colour recreation of a poignant family scene.

The frame around this sign is tin lithographed to simulate wood. Such signs are called "self-framed tin" and are classed as the best of all. This sign advertises a product in the most collectable of all tin categories — tobacco — and it makes an excellent display piece to accompany a collection of Tuckett tins. The portrait of Marguerite, an innocent in Goethe's story of Faust, was painted by A. Asti, whom Tuckett specially commissioned for the work. This is considered the best of all Canadian signs.

Cat. No.	Description	Dimensions	F	G	Ex
S-41	Sunlight Soap canvas	57 x 44	100.00	350.00	500.00
S-42	Tucketts Marguerite tin	46.5 x 72	400.00	1200.00	2000.00

WINCHESTER CIGARETTES

This is believed to be a Canadian sign, featuring a woman of the 1940s holding a flat 50 tin box of cigarettes.

Cat. No.	Description	Dimensions	F	G	Ex
S-43	Winchester celluloid	37 x 41	70.00	140.00	200.00

WINGS

Cat. No.	Description	Dimensions	F	G	Ex
S-44	Wings tin	120 x 44	75.00	150.00	250.00

WOODEN SIGNS

Wooden signs came in all shapes and sizes, and were usually crude affairs. Many of the signs currently found are suspect because of the ease of reproduction. Good wooden trade signs in the shape of the product they promote are very valuable.

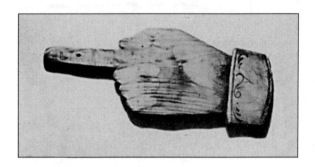

Cat. No.	Description	Dimensions	F	G	Ex
S-45	Wooden Boots	25 x 60	150.00	300.00	500.00
S-46	Wooden Finger	54 x 22	150.00	300.00	500.00
S-47	Wooden Store	116 x 23.5	100.00	200.00	300.00

Tea Tins

British Prime Minister Lloyd George is said to have mentioned to King Edward VII that "the old folk depend on tea for one of their comforts." Evidently it was a dependency that the flood of British immigrants brought with them when they entered the country during the nineteenth century. In most Canadian collections there are about twice as many tea tins as coffee tins.

Tea was always shipped and kept in tin or tin-lined containers. This was necessary in order to keep it as air-tight as possible. Tea leaves were cured in various ways to produce black or green teas, scented or not. You could buy one single type, or a blend. Often the label specified the country of origin.

Sizes of tea tins include large store bins and smaller canisters which the retailer would fill for the customer to take home. Both might have been labelled with the importer's name. By the early twentieth century importers began to pre-package their teas and coffees in ready-to-buy small tins, and the store bins fell out of use.

In coffee and tea tins, top quality is still desired by collectors, but lesser quality tins sell well to decorators because of size, colour, and graphics.

BELFAST BLEND

CAPITOL BLEND
Ceylon Tea Company

Surely this is one of the most beautiful tins ever produced by the Macdonald Manufacturing Company. The picture of the child is printed in paper and then glued to the tin. The scroll work surrounding the picture is lithographed directly on the tin. This is a charming example of the Victorian sentiment for beautiful children. The display lid is another rare feature, with a second inner lid that could be closed to keep the tea air-tight.

There are scenes on each side of this tin from the capitals of Canada and her three closest allies. The top billing — on the long sides — goes to Ottawa and London. We were very proud of our British heritage in those days. Then on the shorter sides — as a supporting cast — are the Capitol in Washington and the Arc de Triomphe in Paris, for the American and French influences.

Cat. No.	Description	Dimensions	F	G	Ex
Tea-1	Belfast Blend	33 x 29 x 34	100.00	250.00	400.00
Tea-2	Capitol Blend	21 x 15 x 18	35.00	80.00	150.00

CHOICE FAMILY TEA

The ship on the front seems to be using both sail and steam. It's a reminder of the early days of the tea trade, when the fastest wooden clipper ships helped to make the fortunes of Maritime shipbuilders. The practice of illustrating four sides of a tin with unrelated pictures is unique to the Macdonald Manufacturing Company in its early years. A tin identical to this is also known to have a Berlin grocer's name stencilled in, instead of "Choice Tea." The other examples of this type are two-colour only. All were made early in the Macdonald career while the company was still at 231 King St. East, Toronto.

Cat. No.	Description	Dimensions	F	G	Ex
Tea-3	Choice Family Tea	18.5 x 25 x 16	30.00	75.00	150.00

GILLARD
W.H. Gillard & Co.

HEAVY DRAUGHT TEA

The Gillard has a busy label, probably a stock design that simply had the wholesaler's name imprinted to order.

This tin is in the same style as the Hillside. Heavy Draught may be the only antique tin to have a pun: draught horses pulling a heavy load on the label, and within a tea that presumably was so good you drank it in "heavy draughts."

Cat. No.	Description	Dimensions	F	G	Ex
Tea-4	Gillard Tea	33 x 33 x 33	50.00	125.00	200.00
Tea-5	Heavy Draught Tea	33 x 33 x 33	75.00	175.00	275.00

HILLSIDE CEYLON TEA
H.B. Hayhoe & Co.

The form of this tea bin, with a half-top lift lid, is characteristic of many. It has a finely-detailed decorative border.

Cat. No.	Description	Dimensions	F	G	Ex
Tea-6	Hillside Ceylon Tea	33 x 33 x 33	50.00	125.00	200.00

HUDSON'S BAY TEA TINS
The Hudson's Bay Company

Four sides of one tin

Hudson's Bay tins are very collectable because of the role the company played in Canadian history. This tin has the bonus of western Canadian scenes on two sides. They are vivid depictions of the optimism and pride in progress which characterized the Edwardian age. One side shows a husky "Jack Canuck" waving to a huge steam tractor pulling three reapers. The other shows a Britannia-like figure, with Canadian coats-of-arms on her shield, enthroned, with an old harvest cradle at her feet and more steam-powered machinery in the background.

Cat. No.	Description	Dimensions	F	G	Ex
Tea-7	Hudson's Bay Tea	15 x 21 x 15	70.00	225.00	400.00

IMPERIAL BLEND
The Imperial Blend Tea Co. Limited

INDIAN & CEYLON BLEND

The Imperial Blend sold in large quantities, making this tin the most common Canadian tea tin.

The "ship" tin was made by the Macdonald Mfg. Co., and an identical one was made by Thomas Davidson for the Ocean Blend Company, see page 135 for an example of this tin.

Cat. No.	Description	Dimensions	F	G	Ex
Tea-8	Imperial Blend Tea	18 x 22 x 12	15.00	25.00	40.00
Tea-9	Imperial Blend Tea	17.5 x 18 x 17.5	20.00	40.00	65.00

INDIAN & CEYLON TEA
The Imperial Blend Tea Co.

MAHARAJAH BLEND

A second, newer style of the "ship" tin for the Indian & Ceylon tea brand from Imperial.

This is one of the earliest Thomas Davidson Co. Ltd. tins.

Cat. No.	Description	Dimensions	F	G	Ex
Tea-10	Imperial Blend Tea	16.5 x 18.5 x 10	15.00	25.00	40.00
Tea-11	Maharajah Blend Tea	33 x 41 x 34	60.00	150.00	250.00

MARSHALL TEA
G. Marshall & Co.

OCEAN BLEND TEA
Ocean Blend Tea Co. Limited

A simple stencilled tin.

The sails are not in sight on these later tins, even though the masts are there. We are into the age that gloried in its steam power.

Cat. No.	Description	Dimensions	F	G	Ex
Tea-12	Marshall Tea	24 x 25 x 24	25.00	50.00	85.00
Tea-13	Ocean Blend Tea	16.5 x 18.5 x 10	15.00	30.00	50.00

RED ROSE TEA
T.H. Estabrook Co. Ltd.

ROSEMARY TEA
Ocean Blend Tea Co. Limited

Red Rose Tea is, of course, still going strong with its familiar red, green and white colours. This tin was sold with contents already packed, rather than being filled in the store from a large bin. This practice gradually became more common as the 20th century advanced.

Cat. No.	Description	Dimensions	F	G	Ex
Tea-14	Red Rose Tea	16 x 23	30.00	50.00	85.00
Tea-15	Rosemary Tea	16.5 x 18.5 x 10	20.00	30.00	45.00

TEA TABLETS
Davis & Lawrence Co. Limited

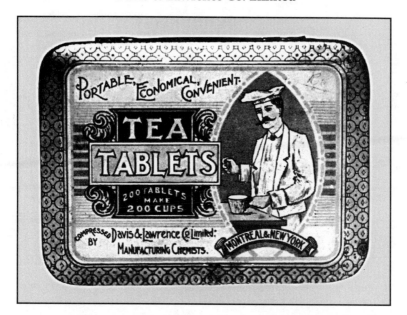

Obviously tea tablets were a bright idea that didn't catch on. They were touted as a "great convenience" for "travellers, campers and miners."

Cat. No.	Description	Dimensions	F	G	Ex
Tea-16	Tea Tablets	12.5 x 9 x 2	15.00	30.00	45.00

Thermometers —Promotional

Thermometers were popular advertising pieces and can still be found on the outside of country stores across Canada. They were practical — each one would collect thousands of glances, making them good investments for the advertiser. Many were made of porcelain because it lasted longer outdoors than any other material.

DR. CHASE'S NERVE FOOD
Kidney-Liver Pills

DR. CHASE'S NERVE FOOD
Syrup of Linseed and Turpentine

This thermometer, advertising Dr. Chase's Linseed, is one of the oldest in Canada. Made of porcelain, it dates from 1915.

Cat. No.	Description	Dimensions	F	G	Ex
Th-1	Kidney-Liver Pills	19 x 97	150.00	300.00	500.00
Th-2	Linseed and Turpentine	19 x 97	150.00	300.00	500.00

COCA-COLA
Coca-Cola Beverages Ltd.

FIVE ROSES

The porcelain Coke thermometers with the silhouette are very desirable because they appeal to both Coke collectors and country store collectors. They come in two different colour designs.

Thermometers were an effective way of keeping the name of a product in the customer's mind. Most brands we find advertised on thermometers still exist today, including the one on this 1930s porcelain thermometer.

Cat. No.	Description	Dimensions	F	G	Ex
Th-3	Coca-Cola	14 x 45.8	250.00	600.00	1000.00+
Th-4	Five Roses	19 x 97	125.00	275.00	400.00

OLD CHUM
Imperial Tobacco Company

ORANGE CRUSH
Orange Crush Ltd.

The Orange Crush tin thermometer features the brown bottle fondly remembered by many.

Cat. No.	Description	Dimensions	F	G	Ex
Th-5	Old Chum, porcelain	19 x 97	70.00	175.00	350.00
Th-6	Orange Crush	15.2 x 48.3	70.00	175.00	350.00

PEG TOP
L.O. Grothe

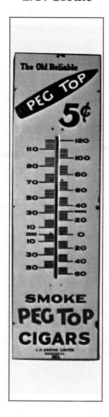

The Peg Top Cigar thermometer is the largest advertising thermometer made. It is very colourful with the cigar and the large 5-cent sign. Advertising that features a price that is now considered outlandishly cheap is very popular.

Cat. No.	Description	Dimensions	F	G	Ex
Th-7	Peg Top, porcelain	37 x 127	150.00	275.00	400.00

Tobacco Tins

Tin collecting is a very specialized field within country store collecting, and in tin collecting itself, tobacco tins are the most sought-after. Tobacco tins can be broken down into various categories according to their shapes. The most popular are the pocket tins, the ones that could fit into a shirt pocket.

After pocket tins, the most collectable are the "square boxes." Despite their varying measurements, the Tonka, the Poker, etc. are "square boxes." The tops of the boxes appear square at first glance and thus the name, even though the correct size is approximately 5 by 4 inches with the depth from just under 2 inches to about 3 inches.

The graphics for the Tonka and the Poker tins show why collecting square boxes is so popular in Canada. Many are extremely attractive. Mooney's Special Mixture is a favourite too, one of the very few Canadian tins to feature a beaver.

Large rectangular boxes for tobacco are called "four by sixes" because of their size. Other than "canisters," which means anything round, this is the last of the descriptive terms for Canadian tobacco tins. For some reason, the Canadian tobacco industry was not fond of "lunchbox" tins, which were popular in the United States (as the name implies, these tins with handles were used as lunchboxes when the tobacco was gone). The only company to use the lunchbox was Empire Tobacco, which produced Great West tobacco. Canadians also generally ignored the flat pocket tins, so named because they were designed to lie flat, and usually could not be stood on end. The "roly-polys," roundish-shaped tins that looked something like a bowling pin, were never manufactured in Canada.

The best of the Canadian pocket tins, the Taxi and the Gold Dust, are acknowledged the world over as two of the best lithographed tins ever made anywhere.

DOMINION TOBACCO CO.
Uncle Sam

EAGLE TOBACCO COMPANY
Saratoga

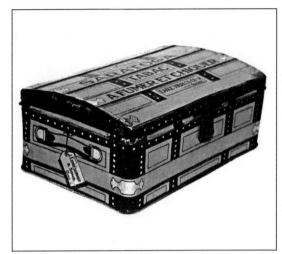

Uncle Sam on a Canadian tin? The Dominion Tobacco Company of Montreal issued this tin between 1910 and 1915. There were a number of Canadian tins produced in the 1910 to 1925 period that had American themes: Old Glory, Chicago Cubs, Seal of North Carolina, Old Virginia, Puritan, and American Navy.

The Saratoga Tobacco is the only tin from the Eagle Tobacco Company. On the back is a lithographed address tag which says, "From J. Lemesurier and Sons, Quebec."

Cat. No.	Description	Dimensions	F	G	Ex
TT-1	Uncle Sam pocket	7.7 x 11	250.00	800.00	1500.00
TT-2	Saratoga box	22.4 x 15 x 8.6	15.00	25.00	50.00

EMPIRE TOBACCO CO.
3 Strikes

Perhaps the earliest of the known Canadian pocket tins, the Three Strikes is also the rarest. Only a few are known to exist. The graphics suggest an 1895 date, coincident with the existence of the Empire Tobacco Company of Granby, Quebec, which is thought to be what the E.T. Co. on the batter's chest stands for. "Manly" themes like sports and fishing are popular in tobacco tin collecting, which adds to this tin's appeal. There is no manufacturer's mark, but the tin's base bears information relating to "the statutes of Canada."

Cat. No.	Description	Dimensions	F	G	Ex
TT-3	3 Strikes pocket	7.7 x 10.8	750.00	2500.00+	5000.00+

HICKEY AND NICHOLSON

Perique

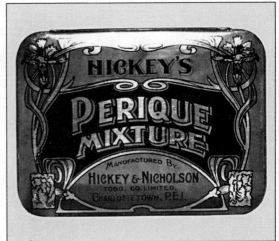

The Hickey and Nicholson Tobacco Company of Charlottetown, P.E.I. seems to have been the only Maritime company to produce tins in any quantity. In recent years a large number of near-mint condition tins have appeared, probably the result of a warehouse find.

Cat. No.	Description	Dimensions	F	G	Ex
TT-4	Hickey and Nicholson box	12.7 x 9.3 x 4.8	10.00	20.00	35.00
TT-5	Hickey's Perique box	12.7 x 9.3 x 4.8	10.00	20.00	35.00

HICKEY AND NICHOLSON
Rival Twist

HUDSON'S BAY COMPANY
Imperial Mixture

Rival Twist is another of the Hickey & Nicholson brands from Charlottetown, P.E.I.

Hudson's Bay Co. Imperial Mixture came in a variety of shapes and sizes, all collectable because of the historic significance of the company. They are more popular in western Canada.

Cat. No.	Description	Dimensions	F	G	Ex
TT-6	Rival Twist box	18.4 x 16.3 x 7.6	10.00	25.00	40.00
TT-7	Hudson's Bay canister	8.4 x 4.3	10.00	30.00	50.00

B. HOUDE AND COMPANY

Champaign

Golden Leaf

B. Houde and Co. were the giants of the tobacco industry in the early 1900s. Two of its brands, the Senator and the Champaign, were quite popular.

The Golden Leaf tin bears one of the earliest registered tin designs in Canada, 1898 according to the tin. The B. Houde Co. started business in 1841 and by 1898 was the largest tobacco manufacturer in Canada.

Cat. No.	Description	Dimensions	F	G	Ex
TT-8	Champaign box	12.5 x 9.3 x 7.5	25.00	70.00	100.00
TT-9	Golden Leaf box	12.7 x 9.4 x 7.4	25.00	60.00	100.00

B. HOUDE AND COMPANY

Horseshoe Solace

Houde's No. 1

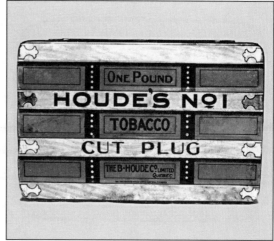

The L.L. inside the horseshoe refers to the L.L. Larue Jr. Co. bought out by Houde. The tin is very common.

This tin and the Saratoga are both shaped and lithographed like little trunks, complete with latch at the front. Perhaps meant to be given as presents, both tins are from "The Thos Davidson Mfg. Co. Limited, Montreal, Tin Boxes."

Cat. No.	Description	Dimensions	F	G	Ex
TT-10	Horseshoe Solace box	15.5 x 10.5 x 6.3	10.00	25.00	45.00
TT-11	Houde's No. 1 box	22.4 x 15 x 8.6	10.00	25.00	40.00

B. HOUDE AND COMPANY

O.K Smoking Tobacco

Senator Smoking Tobacco

This is the common variation of the O.K. Smoking Tobacco. A rarer design features a woman's head inside the horseshoe.

Cat. No.	Description	Dimensions	F	G	Ex
TT-12	O.K. box	12.5 x 9.3 x 4.5	10.00	20.00	30.00
TT-13	Senator box	12.5 x 9.3 x 7.5	15.00	25.00	40.00

IMPERIAL TOBACCO COMPANY

Calabash Canister   **Calabash Flip-Top Pocket**

The Calabash with the flip-top lid was produced by Imperial Tobacco Co. of Montreal. These lids were used in Canada on just three pockets: the Calabash, the Regal, and the magnificent Taxi. The Calabash bears the inscription "Patent Applied For," so is presumably the oldest of the three flip-tops. The brown colouring and shading is intended to simulate leather.

Cat. No.	Description	Dimensions	F	G	Ex
TT-14	Calabash canister	8.4 x 4.4	20.00	50.00	75.00
TT-15	Calabash flip-top pocket	8.7 x 10.2	50.00	150.00	250.00

IMPERIAL TOBACCO COMPANY

Forest & Stream   Forest & Stream

 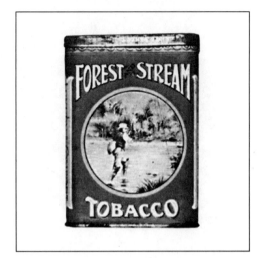

The Forest and Stream is probably the most collectable series of tins in Canada. Most use a full-colour lithograph of a fishing scene on a bright red background. Both the theme and the variety of tins available make it a favourite series. The hardest two to find are the "two fishermen in a canoe" pocket and vacuum-sealed canister.

The single fisherman tin is a good example of how rarity can become commonplace overnight. A few years ago the tin listed at a high price in an American price guide, and then forty of the tins were found in a barn in Norwich, Ontario, and another twenty in a garage in Quebec and down came the price. The tins are circa 1915.

Cat. No.	Description	Dimensions	F	G	Ex
TT-16	Forest & Stream pocket	7.7 x 10.5	60.00	175.00	300.00
TT-17	Forest & Stream pocket	7.7 x 10.5	25.00	60.00	100.00

IMPERIAL TOBACCO COMPANY

Forest & Stream   Forest & Stream

The screw top marks this canister as quite modern by tin collecting standards, but the fact that it belongs to the popular Forest and Stream set makes it collectable anyway.

Cat. No.	Description	Dimensions	F	G	Ex
TT-18	Forest & Stream Duck pocket	7.7 x 10	15.00	25.00	40.00
TT-19	Forest & Stream Duck canister	11 x 10.7	10.00	25.00	40.00

IMPERIAL TOBACCO COMPANY
Forest & Stream

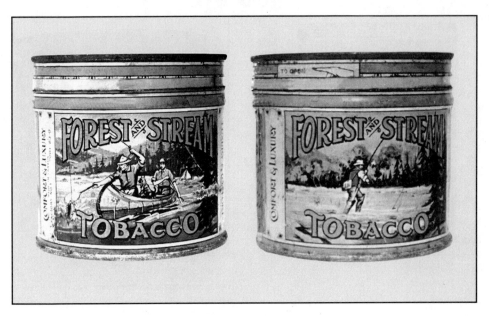

Two sides of the very rare vacuum-sealed canister.

Cat. No.	Description	Dimensions	F	G	Ex
TT-20	Forest & Stream canister	11 x 10	100.00	300.00	750.00

IMPERIAL TOBACCO COMPANY

Gold Dust

King Edward

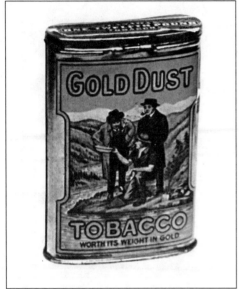

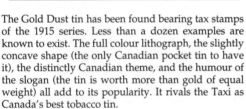

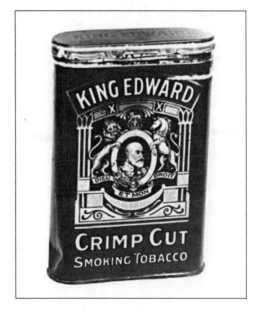

The Gold Dust tin has been found bearing tax stamps of the 1915 series. Less than a dozen examples are known to exist. The full colour lithograph, the slightly concave shape (the only Canadian pocket tin to have it), the distinctly Canadian theme, and the humour of the slogan (the tin is worth more than gold of equal weight) all add to its popularity. It rivals the Taxi as Canada's best tobacco tin.

Edward VII was an immensely popular monarch. His picture graces many Canadian products. The royalty theme or the word "regal" occurs on at least a dozen containers made in the Edwardian era, 1901 to 1910.

Cat. No.	Description	Dimensions	F	G	Ex
TT-21	Gold Dust pocket	7.7 x 10.8	750.00	2000.00	3000.00+
TT-22	King Edward pocket	7.7 x 11	100.00	250.00	450.00

IMPERIAL TOBACCO COMPANY

Old Chum

Regal

The Regal is one of a series of "royalty" tobacco tins used in Canada. Others with this theme are the King Edward, King George's Navy, Royal Navy, British Consul, and Prince of Wales.

Cat. No.	Description	Dimensions	F	G	Ex
TT-23	Old Chum box	9.5 x 12 x 6	10.00	20.00	30.00
TT-24	Regal flip-top pocket	8.7 x 10.2	50.00	150.00	250.00

IMPERIAL TOBACCO COMPANY

Repeater   Social Mixture

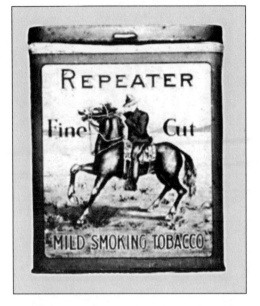

This tin is popular because of its picture of a Mountie shooting his "repeater" rifle. It came in a variety of sizes.

Cat. No.	Description	Dimensions	F	G	Ex
TT-25	Repeater box	9.5 x 12 x 6	20.00	50.00	75.00
TT-26	Social Mixture box	9 x 12.4 x 6	10.00	25.00	40.00

IMPERIAL TOBACCO COMPANY

Taxi

Velvet

The Taxi is probably the most beautiful tin ever designed. It was issued by the Imperial Tobacco Company, meaning it was made after 1906, but it is unmarked as to manufacturer. It exists in at least three variations, with differences in the words at the bottom, but no changes in the remarkable graphics.

This is a common Canadian tin. The Velvet is identical to an American tin except for the inscription on the side: "Manufactured by Imperial Tobacco Company of Canada Limited successor to Spaulding and Merrick" (American concerns).

Cat. No.	Description	Dimensions	F	G	Ex
TT-27	Taxi pocket	7.7 x 11	750.00	2000.00	3000.00-
TT-28	Velvet pocket	8 x 10.5	5.00	10.00	20.00

LANDAU & CORMACK
3 Twins

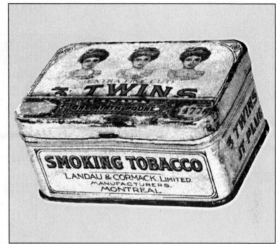

This is a pleasant tin with its basic yellow colouring and the full-colour triplets. It is not easy to find.

Even though the surface area of the top of this tiny 3 Twins is one-third of the larger one, the illustration of the girls remains the same size.

Cat. No.	Description	Dimensions	F	G	Ex
TT-29	3 Twins box	16.7 x 10.2 x 5.4	25.00	75.00	125.00
TT-30	3 Twins box	9.7 x 6.3 x 4.4	25.00	40.00	75.00

W.C. MACDONALD COMPANY
Napoleon Honey Dew

Even though the W. C. MacDonald Co. was in business from 1858 until recently, when R.J. Reynolds took it over, MacDonald marketed very few memorable tobacco tins. The Napoleon is one of the few. It was available also in a smaller size.

Cat. No.	Description	Dimensions	F	G	Ex
TT-31	Napoleon canister	13 x 10.5	15.00	30.00	45.00

W.C. MACDONALD COMPANY
Pilot Chewing Tobacco

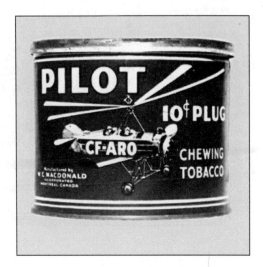 

These W.C. MacDonald Pilot tins are from the 1930s, with the autogiro being older than the plane.

Cat. No.	Description	Dimensions	F	G	Ex
TT-32	Autogiro	13 x 10.3	30.00	60.00	100.00
TT-33	Plane	13 x 10.7	20.00	50.00	75.00

MCALPIN TOBACCO COMPANY
Tonka Mixture

E.A. MORRIS
Morris' Special Smoking Mixture

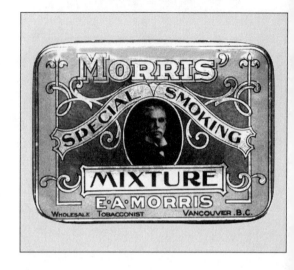

The Tonka seems to be the only tin issued by the McAlpin Tobacco Company of Toronto. The tin claims that "the formula of this mixture is largely used by British Officers in India and has no equal." It dates from about 1895.

Very few tobacco tins come from west coast companies. The Morris company is responsible for a majority of those.

Cat. No.	Description	Dimensions	F	G	Ex
TT-34	Tonka tin	12.8 x 9.4 x 8	30.00	60.00	125.00
TT-35	Morris' tin	12.7 x 9.4 x 7.4	25.00	60.00	100.00

ROCK CITY TOBACCO CO. LIMITED
American Navy   Check

The Rock City Tobacco Company of Quebec seemed fascinated with the Navy theme. As well as American Navy, it sold King George Navy, World Navy, Navy Plug, Britannia and Torpedo tobacco. The company was formed in 1899 and took its name from Quebec City's fortress-like position above the St. Lawrence River.

The building on the Check cigar canister is the home of the Rock City Cigar Co. in Levis, Quebec, a subsidiary of the Rock City Tobacco Company.

Cat. No.	Description	Dimensions	F	G	Ex
TT-36	American Navy box	16 x 11 x 7.3	20.00	40.00	75.00
TT-37	Check canister	13.3 x 12.5	20.00	50.00	75.00

ROCK CITY TOBACCO CO. LIMITED
Kodak Smoking Tobacco

The Kodak design was registered in 1899 by the Macdonald Manufacturing Company, but someone evidently forgot to check the trademark files thoroughly enough. According to John Sebert in *Tin Type* magazine, the appearance of the name Kodak on a tobacco tin "had George Eastman and his newly-formed film company rushing to the courts to stamp out this Canadian upstart." The Kodak tin is rare; apparently the film company was successful in defending its prior claim.

Cat. No.	Description	Dimensions	F	G	Ex
TT-38	Kodak	12.5 x 9 x 4	30.00	75.00	125.00

ROCK CITY TOBACCO CO. LIMITED
Master Mason

The Master Mason pocket tin dates from about 1915. It is one of just two pockets put out by Rock City. The graphic shows a mason holding his square and some plugs of Master Mason chewing tobacco — a square deal. Rock City issued four other tins with the Master Mason brand, but they lack any distinction in style or colour.

The Master Mason canister is very bland.

Cat. No.	Description	Dimensions	F	G	Ex
TT-39	Master Mason pocket	7.7 x 11	250.00	650.00	1200.00
TT-40	Master Mason canister	13.3 x 6.8	10.00	20.00	30.00

ROCK CITY TOBACCO CO. LIMITED
Poker Cut Plug

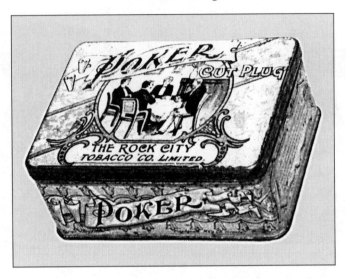

Cat. No.	Description	Dimensions	F	G	Ex
TT-41	Poker box	11 x 7.7 x 4.5	50.00	150.00	250.00

ROCK CITY TOBACCO CO. LTD.
World's Navy

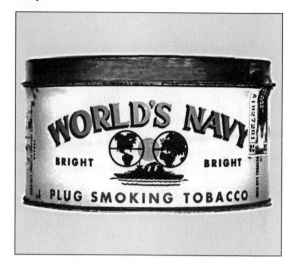

World's Navy is one of Rock City's navy themes, and is one of the most common Canadian tobacco tins.

Cat. No.	Description	Dimensions	F	G	Ex
TT-42	World's Navy box	18.4 x 16.3 x 6.3	10.00	20.00	30.00
TT-43	World's Navy canister	15 x 8.3	10.00	20.00	30.00

ROYAL CANADIAN TOBACCO CO.
Silver Dollar

THE TUCKETT TOBACCO COMPANY
Abbey

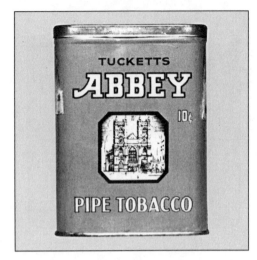

The Silver Dollar is a later tobacco tin, probably issued in the 1930s, from the Royal Canadian Tobacco Company, of Toronto.

Most tobacco companies made their pocket tins the most attractive. The Tuckett Tobacco Company of Hamilton is the exception. Both the Abbey and the Old Squire are singularly lacking in appeal. The Abbey features a black and white drawing of Hamilton's abbey, which is still standing and in use.

Cat. No.	Description	Dimensions	F	G	Ex
TT-44	Silver Dollar canister	10.8 x 7.8	10.00	20.00	30.00
TT-45	Abbey pocket	7.7 x 10	35.00	75.00	150.00

THE TUCKETT TOBACCO COMPANY
Old Squire

Cat. No.	Description	Dimensions	F	G	Ex
TT-46	Old Squire Pocket	7.7 x 10	35.00	75.00	150.00

THE TUCKETT TOBACCO COMPANY
Orinoco

The Tuckett Orinoco is unusual because usually the best graphics on a 4 by 6 occur on the top. Here the enchanting scene of a man fishing (in the Orinoco River?) has been printed on the side. The dog between his legs must be related to Nipper, the RCA Victor dog.

There are about twenty variations of this tin. Notice the difference in graphics, particularly the fish instead of the Tuckett's tin beside the man on this newer tin.

Cat. No.	Description	Dimensions	F	G	Ex
TT-47	Orinoco box	16.5 x 10.2 x 10	25.00	50.00	75.00
TT-48	Orinoco box	9 x 7 x 4	15.00	30.00	50.00

THE TUCKETT TOBACCO COMPANY
T &B

ANDREW WILSON & CO. LTD.
Humber

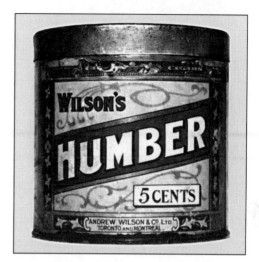

These tiny boxes held from one sixth to one ninth of a pound of tobacco. The T & B stands for Tuckett and Billings, early partners.

A 1920s version of the cigar canister.

Cat. No.	Description	Dimensions	F	G	Ex
TT-49	T & B Renowned box	9 x 7 x 5	10.00	25.00	40.00
TT-50	Humber canister	12.7 x 13	20.00	50.00	75.00

ALIVE BOLLARD

BLACK FOX

Taller than the other little canisters, the Alive Bollard tin is an example of a private brand tin.

This tin was made by the Heekin Can Co. of Cincinnati, Ohio, and dates from the 1920s. To be complete it must have the fully-lithographed lid.

Cat. No.	Description	Dimensions	F	G	Ex
TT-51	Alive Bollard canister	8.4 x 7.3	20.00	40.00	60.00
TT-52	Black Fox canister	13.2 x 13.2	100.00	450.00	700.00

A. CLUBB & SONS
Clubb's Dollar Mixture

W.J. CLUBB
Clubb's Perique

Cat. No.	Description	Dimensions	F	G	Ex
TT-53	Clubb's Dollar box	16.5 x 10.5 x 5.5	10.00	20.00	35.00
TT-54	Clubb's Perique box	16.5 x 10 x 5.5	25.00	75.00	125.00

Note: It is thought that W.J. Clubb was one of the sons mentioned in the Toronto Clubb's tin.

J. ERZINGER
Erzinger's Smoking Mixture

ESKIMO
Smoking Tobacco

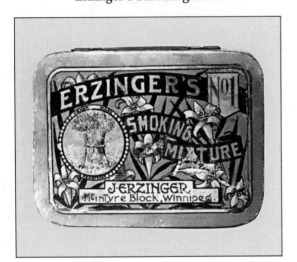

The Erzinger's is a very colourful tin from Winnipeg. The pocket tin is very hard to find.

The Eskimo tin is desirable because of the large animal picture.

Cat. No.	Description	Dimensions	F	G	Ex
TT-55	Erzinger's box	12.5 x 9.3 x 4.5	30.00	60.00	100.00
TT-56	Eskimo canister	11 x 15	50.00	200.00	350.00

GOLDSTEIN'S MIXTURE

No other tins from this company have been found. The tin was manufactured by Thos. Davidson of Montreal.

Cat. No.	Description	Dimensions	F	G	Ex
TT-57	Goldstein's Mixture box	15.5 x 10.5 x 12.2	15.00	30.00	45.00

IRVING CIGARS

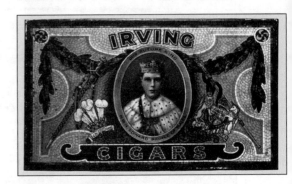

Both tins are stunning in their use of full colour, yet both are, surprisingly, unmarked as to manufacturer. The cigars are from J. Hirsch and Sons, of Montreal. It seems, from the inside lithography (lower) , that the name of the cigars is a tribute to Washington Irving, the American author.

Cat. No.	Description	Dimensions	F	G	Ex
TT-58	Coronation	21 x 12.3 x 3.5	20.00	40.00	75.00
TT-59	Future King	21 x 12.3 x 3.5	20.00	40.00	75.00

JOS. DOUVILLE

LAURIER

Cat. No.	Description	Dimensions	F	G	Ex
TT-60	Jos. Douville box	16.5 x 10.3 x 6.4	10.00	20.00	30.00
TT-61	Laurier cigar box	26 x 15	20.00	30.00	45.00

W.J. MOONEY
Mooney's Special Smoking Mixture

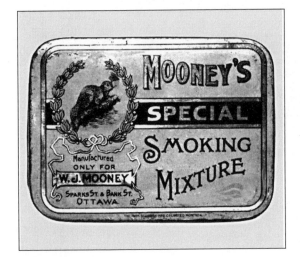

D. RITCHIE & CO.
St. Leger Flake Smoking Tobacco

This tin is probably one of the earliest lithographed tins made for the Canadian market. It was manufactured by Somers Bros. of Brooklyn, N.Y., and the design was patented April 29, 1879. Canadian firms switched from stencilling to lithography a few years after this. This tin, with several flakes of paint chipped off, is probably in the least acceptable condition for a collector.

Cat. No.	Description	Dimensions	F	G	Ex
TT-62	Mooney's box	12.7 x 9.3 x 7.5	20.00	50.00	90.00
TT-63	St. Leger Flake Cut box	12.7 x 9.5 x 4.8	30.00	70.00	150.00

WINNER SMOKING TOBACCO

An extremely rare tin from Western Canada.

Cat. No.	Description	Dimensions	F	G	Ex
TT-64	Winner canister	14 x 7	70.00	250.00	400.00

Miscellaneous

There are literally thousands of miscellaneous collectables from country stores. Country store collectables can include anything that was once in a general store, is pleasant to look at, attractive enough to display, or the kind of thing people like to wonder about.

A.K. MAINSPRINGS
Albert Kleiser

A factory on a miniature. The tin is unusual because very, very few tins were lithographed on the bottom.

Cat. No.	Description	Dimensions	F	G	Ex
Misc-1	A.K. Mainsprings	7 x 7	10.00	20.00	30.00

BLACK CAT
The Nonsuch Mfg. Co. Limited

Besides calendars, companies gave away dozens of advertising items — fans, mugs, buttons, pocket mirrors, letter openers, book marks, toys, and other gimmicks. This Black Cat piece is a bill-holder, hence the wicked-looking hook. Note that the sign around the cat's neck says, "The black cat brings good luck." That's the English version of the common superstition.

Cat. No.	Description	Dimensions	F	G	Ex
Misc-2	Black Cat Bill Holder	9 x 17	60.00	175.00	300.00

PEABODY'S RAG DOLL
Peabody Company

The Peabody Jeans rag doll cut-out came free if you mailed a certificate found in the pocket of every pair of jeans. The Peabody Company of Walkerville, Ontario, was proud of its relationship with its workers. It declared their overalls were "worth their weight in HONEST WAGES," and were made "by well-paid and fairly-treated employees." The item is c. 1910.

Cat. No.	Description	Dimensions	F	G	Ex
Misc-3	Peabody's Rag Doll	61 x 45	60.00	125.00	200.00

ALFRED TYLER

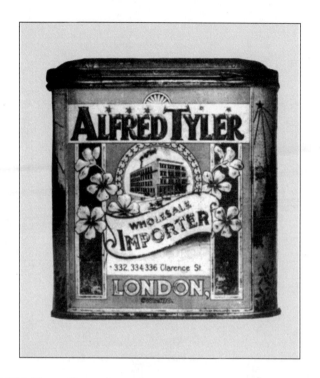

Cat. No.	Description	Dimensions	F	G	Ex
Misc-4	Tyler's	21 x 21.5	30.00	60.00	100.00

INDEX

NOSTALGIA-RAMA ® '97
EST. 1976

S N A C K B A R

F R E E P A R K I N G

SOUTHERN ONTARIO'S LARGEST
SMALL ANTIQUES, NOSTALGIA AND COLLECTABLES SHOW

AUDITORIUM • FAIRGROUNDS
WOODSTOCK ONTARIO

MAR. 9, JUNE 22, SEPT. 7, NOV. 9 1997

HOURS 10AM to 4PM

85 DEALERS — 180 TABLES
FROM ONTARIO & QUEBEC

SOME FEATURING

Country Store Items, Rec Room And Restaurant Decor, Dye Cabinets, Old Calendars, Canadiana Historical Items, Documents, Tins, Militaria, Antiques, Brewenana, Dolls, Souvenir Spoons, Antique Glassware, Store Signs, Automobilia, Depression Glass, Postcards, Old Toys, Bottles, Prints, Coins, Stereographs, Pulp Magazines, Railroad Items, Coke Items, Sports Cards, Time Pieces, Paper Ephemera, Sheet Music, Old Tools, Salt & Pepper, Old Advertising Posters, Licence Plates, Telephone Memorabilia, 1950s Big Band Posters, Art Deco, Hunting & Fishing Memorabilia, Old Lace, Old Photos, Medals, Badges, Collectors Plates, Antique Reference Books, Crocks, And Many More Unusual Items.

**MOST OF THE ABOVE ITEMS BOUGHT AND SOLD BY PARTICIPATING DEALERS
DEALER ENQUIRIES: BILL LAVELL 1301 AMBLESIDE DR.,
MISSISSAUGA, ONT. L5H 1N7 TEL: (905) 278-7363 FAX: (905) 278-4971
REGRET: NO ARTS & CRAFTS AND NO "EARLY BIRD" ADMISSIONS**

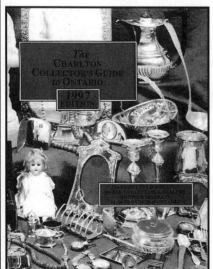

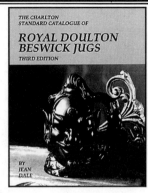

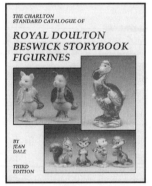